Reclaimed Joy

Discovering the God of Wonders in Your Whys

By Lisa Jennings

Reclaimed Joy
© 2022 by Lisa Jennings

This title is also available in Kindle format.

Published with help from 100X Publishing
Olympia, Washington | www.100Xacademy.com

All rights reserved. No part of this publication may be reproduced, stored in a retrieval system, or transmitted in any form or by any means--for example, electronic, photocopy, recording--without the prior written permission of the publisher.
Holy Bible, New International Version®, NIV®: Copyright ©1973, 1978, 1984, 2011 by Biblica, Inc.® Used by permission. All rights reserved worldwide.
The Living Bible copyright © 1971 by Tyndale House Foundation. Used by permission of Tyndale House Publishers Inc., Carol Stream, Illinois 60188. All rights reserved.
Amplified Bible, Classic Edition (AMPC): Copyright © 1954, 1958, 1962, 1964, 1965, 1987 by The Lockman Foundation.
The Passion Translation® (TPT). Copyright © 2017, 2018, 2020 by Passion & Fire Ministries, Inc. Used by permission. All rights reserved. thePassionTranslation.com.
The Message (MSG): Copyright © 1993, 2002, 2018 by Eugene H. Peterson.
GOD'S WORD Translation (GW): Copyright © 1995, 2003, 2013, 2014, 2019, 2020 by God's Word to the Nations Mission Society. All rights reserved.

ISBN: 979-8-9856830-0-4

"Over the course of 20 years in ministry, I have heard the most horrifying stories of abuse and trauma that honestly take my breath away. Some of these women tell their stories of how God healed their broken hearts, while others bury their faces in my chest with tears, just starting their journey of trusting God to heal them. When some of these brave warriors choose to print their story, I carry great admiration for them. You see, Lisa, and many other courageous souls, have chosen to give others their vulnerable stories in exchange for even just one soul to be miraculously touched by the unfailing love of God. These authors are rescuers, plain and simple. They are heroes of the faith. Maybe you, too, will share your story one day and set another person free. But for now, if you have experienced pain that is so deep, you can feel your heart twisted into a knot, let Lisa's words unwrap your tender soul and lead you to the oasis of healing."

Jenny Donnelly
Author, Founder of Her Voice Movement

Dedication

This book is dedicated to the Healer of souls, Jesus, who without His love I would not know true freedom.

To my husband whose love is limitless when I tested the limits.

To my sons who have shown love and forgiveness
in the most trying circumstances.

To all the lovely people in my life who have prayed, loved, and helped me live whole in the shadow of the cross. My heart is eternally grateful to walk this path with you.

And to all the beautiful people who have more *whys* than answers.
May you find comfort here.

Table of Contents

Introduction 9

Chapter 1: Formed By His Wonder 11

Chapter 2: Reclaiming Joy 30

Chapter 3: Whoville 40

Chapter 4: Medley Of Satan's Greatest Hits 58

Chapter 5: The Not-So-Funhouse Mirror 69

Chapter 6: You Do You, Boo 82

Chapter 7: Never Enough 96

Chapter 8: Shame On You 109

Chapter 9: Forgiveness Takes Courage 125

Chapter 10: Closed Door, Opened Window 138

Final Thoughts: Healing's Patchwork Quilt 161

Reclaimed

The Lord Reclaimed You

Isaiah 44:24 (GW)

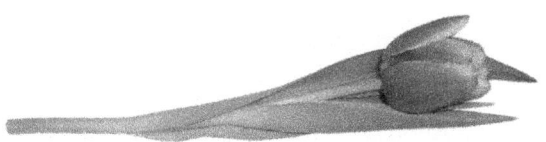

I absolutely love to celebrate! Name the occasion, and I'll find the matching napkins, paper plates, and of course, the goodie bags! The name of these small bags of treasures says it all – *goodie*. I feel the same way about the word *reclaimed*; it is so power-packed with God's goodness, the mere mention of it can take your breath away. And for good reason. Merriam-Webster dictionary describes it as *get back, re-collect, recapture, recover, regain, repossess, retake, retrieve, redeem, replenish, repurchase, rescue.* It goes on to say that reclaim suggests a *bringing back to a former state or condition of someone or something abandoned or debased.* And if you, like me, have ever suffered trauma of any kind, these afflictions can leave gaping holes in your heart.

These empty spaces can feel unredeemable, a loss so intense they are unable to be restored. Yet we have a God in the business of reclaiming our lives with joy, bursting onto the scene to rescue us, no matter how messy or broken we are. He brings His full redemption, which is never too late and always right on time. Where the enemy once riddled us with shame, guilt, and heartbreak, punching holes in our heart, fragmenting our life story, when it's yielded to God, it is gloriously transformed into celebratory confetti. Our messes become miracles, sorrow erupting into full-blown joy, and our newfound freedom becomes a genuine celebration. When accepting the invitation to party with Jesus, we may gather as broken, but we leave completely whole and filled to the brim with joy.

With this book, my prayer for you is to behold the God of wonders in your *whys*, seeing with wide-eyed wonderment all that God has reclaimed in your life. With that comes total freedom and wholeness, giving you the ability to gaze wholly into the crystal-clear revelation of just how much your heavenly Father loves you unequivocally. Always has, always will.

And that, my friend, calls for a huge celebration. Remember to bring your confetti.

Chapter 1

Formed By His Wonder

The Lord Formed You

"You formed my innermost being, shaping my delicate inside and my intricate outside, and wove them all together in my mother's womb."
—Psalm 139:13 (TPT)

"Lord, you delivered me safely from my mother's womb. You are the one who cared for me ever since I was a baby. Since the day I was born, I've been placed in your custody. You've cradled me throughout my days, and you've always been my God."
—Psalm 22:9-10 (TPT)

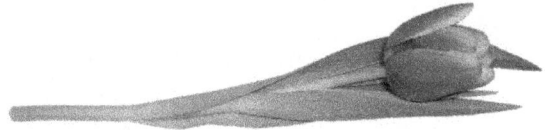

Hello, World

My first glimpse of the world was on July 17th, 1961 – all nine pounds and half an ounce of me. Sorry about that, Mom. However, I was not the only weight my mom carried those nine months. For within her belly brewed the perfect storm: foreboding fear, triggered by my mother's previous loss, produced not only waves of sorrow, but heart palpitations that lasted the rest of her life. Nestled in her womb, I became a roommate of trauma, with more traumatic events to follow in my growing up years.

I understand the validity of my mom carrying trauma, having conceived me only three short months after my parents laid their ten-month-old baby boy to rest in the Spring Water Cemetery in Estacada, Oregon (the final resting place for a large portion of my mom's side of the family).

A simple hernia operation left their precious son dead, never waking up from the anesthesia. The last time my mom saw her son, doctors and nurses were frantically working on him to start his heart by massaging it and packing him in ice. She ran out of the hospital room, never to hold him again. A simple procedure went tragically wrong.

Some doctors believed perhaps it may have been the anesthesia that Brent had a reaction to. My mom had a scare as a young adult while her wisdom teeth were being pulled. She clearly remembered, while sedated, seeing a little gnome-like creature, the likes of the Travelocity mascot. This gnome's travel was restricted to walking around a clock, repeating the phrase, "We won't wake up," over and over again. The theory that anesthesia could have caused Brent's death had my mom hyper-vigilant, doing everything in her power to make sure we would never have it. Medical alert bracelets were my fashion statements for years.

So, grief took up residence as an unwanted guest, got comfy and wore out its welcome...though it was never wanted in the first place. One thing my mom did was to press hard into God, just like she always had when her pain was unbearable and during the whys of her numbing loss. The Lord was there at grief's every twist and turn with consolation, filling her bone-dry emotional cup with His life-giving water.

A Birthday Surprise

Shortly into her grief journey, something birthed in my mom's spirit that took her by surprise: a deep desire to become pregnant again. My brother Troy was three at the time and was grappling with the loss of his brother in his own limited understanding. He would talk to Brent as if he was still there, playing alongside him, telling him he would be okay. Brent was okay, for he now played with the angels, but Troy was too young to fully understand where his little buddy had gone.

Mom's desire to have another baby became a reality, landing her smack dab in the hospital right on Brent's birthday, July 17th. When she would have been celebrating his birthday, she celebrated mine too. I was fashionably late in accordance to Dr. Ricker's predictions of my due date. Back in those days, they let nature take its course, meaning the mamas were more miserable for longer. My mom would chat with her mother, puzzled before my birth, wondering, "Surely this baby could not come on Brent's birthday?" Surely, I did. Ta-da! Not only did I come on his birthday, I did so in the same hospital and same room (471-C) that Brent graced the world in. For kicks and giggles, the Lord also had the same doctor and nurse on duty.

Divine Appointment

How's that for a divine appointment, with all the bells and whistles, just in case you missed the significance of what God was doing? I am reminded of this glorious thanksgiving in Psalm (118:21-25 MSG). "Thank you for responding to me; you've truly become my salvation! This is God's work. We rub our eyes – we can hardly believe it! This is the very day God acted - let's celebrate and be festive." The Message Bible says in Psalm 118:27, "Festoon the shrine with garlands, hang colored banners above the altar..."

"This is God's work."

My mom not only celebrated my special day with awe and wonder, it also spoke volumes to her broken heart of the faithfulness of God. The timing of my birth both showed the underlying truth of His love and faithfulness to my mom and created an anchor for my tempest-tossed soul. Throughout my life when pitch black thoughts of suicide darkened my thinking, a light would burst through because of this anchor, reminding me I mattered and had a purpose even if I could not see or feel it.

To this day, whenever my husband and I see 7:17 on the clock or anywhere else it might pop up, we declare, "It's my birthday! This funny game we play has underlined my value when lack of self-worth was determined to knock me down. For all of us, can we ever celebrate the day of our birth too much or ponder how valued we are by God? I think not! We can celebrate! God thinks you're a really big deal.

We all matter and carry within us a God-given purpose no matter what day we were born or the circumstances surrounding it.

Even with all our celebrations and the revelation of our purpose, we can still carry trauma from the womb. Jesus wants to heal it. Studies show children between birth to age five are the most vulnerable to the effects of trauma, since their brains are still in the early formative years (lookthroughtheireyes.org). I will touch on this a little later in the book. In the end, it is my prayer you will have the ability to see yourself in a place of total redemption.

That, my friend, is good news! As we look at Psalm 139, God's victorious truth reveals His pure love and devotion to us even before conception. Allow His truth to shed new light and bring deeper healing; ponder the declaration that He not only knows all about you...He is madly in love with you.

I'm feeling better already.

You Know All About Me

"Lord, You know everything there is to know about me.
You perceive every movement of my heart and soul,
and You understand my every thought before it even enters my mind.
You are so intimately aware of me, Lord.
You read my heart like an open book,
and You know all the words I'm about to speak
before I even start a sentence!
You know every step I will take before my journey even begins.
You've gone into my future to prepare the way,
and in kindness, You follow behind me

to spare me from the harm of my past.
With Your hand of love upon my life,
You impart a blessing to me.
This is just too wonderful, deep, and incomprehensible!
Your understanding of me brings me wonder and strength.
Where could I go from Your Spirit?
Where could I run and hide from Your face?
If I go up to heaven, You're there!
If I go down to the realm of the dead, You're there too!
If I fly with wings into the shining dawn, You're there!
If I fly into the radiant sunset, You're there waiting!
Wherever I go, Your hand will guide me;
Your strength will empower me.
It's impossible to disappear from You
or to ask the darkness to hide me,
for Your presence is everywhere, bringing light into my night.
There is no such thing as darkness with You.
The night, to You, is as bright as the day;
there's no difference between the two.
You formed my innermost being, shaping my delicate inside
and my intricate outside,
and wove them all together in my mother's womb.
I thank You, God, for making me so mysteriously complex!
Everything You do is marvelously breathtaking.
It simply amazes me to think about it!
How thoroughly You know me, Lord!
You even formed every bone in my body
when You created me in the secret place,
carefully, skillfully shaping me from nothing to something.
You saw who You created me to be before I became me!
Before I'd ever seen the light of day,
the number of days You planned for me
was already recorded in Your book.
Every single moment, You are thinking of me!
How precious and wonderful to consider

that You cherish me constantly in Your every thought!
O God, Your desires toward me are more
than the grains of sand on every shore!
When I awake each morning, You're still with me."
—Psalm 139:1-18 TPT

Unloved To Beloved

Let that poetic promise sink deep down into your spirit, settling in your heart and mind. The Creator of the universe is your Papa Daddy. He's scheduling your days, skillfully shaping you from nothing into something. Perhaps, at times, you feel like you're nothing, a nobody; however, your loving Father God says quite the contrary.

God's Word declares, "I'll call nobodies and make them somebodies. I'll call the unloved and make them beloved. In the place where they yelled out 'You're nobody!' they're calling you 'God's living children'" (Romans 9:25-26, MSG).

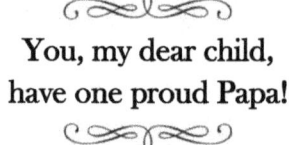

You, my dear child, have one proud Papa who is grinning from ear to ear over you. His lavish, never-ending love beams like the sun.

You, my dear child, have one proud Papa!

God's glorious creation resides in you. Divinities sparked at the moment of your conception. In fact, scientists can now capture the flash of light that sparks when the sperm meets the egg. Way before you were a gleam in your earthly father's eye, you were a gleam your Heavenly Father's (Sciencealert.com).

First Trick Of The Enemy

You might be well aware of how the devil tries to steal our life and joy right from conception. His resume is filled with destruction and hearty referrals of jobs well done. He does not just want your joy; he wants your identity, your God-breathed soul. He is so eager to destroy the unborn before God's creation is complete. He is determined to see that God's knitting in a mother's womb ceases and the clicking of God's hard-working knitting needles goes silent.

My heart breaks with such grief whenever I remember going with my friend to get an abortion, thinking I was helping her. I could not have been any further from the truth. Twice in my life, I was almost confronted with the same decision, i.e., when I recall my sexual encounters at 15 and rape at 17. My heart was so broken and callused, buying into so many lies. I lost sight of God's truth that life begins at conception.

As I write this in tears, I'm so thankful for a God who sees our pain, loves us in all our brokenness. He is a God full and overflowing with compassion, forgiveness, and abounding grace. God longs for us to walk in complete victory and unlimited freedom, coming alongside us to remove anything that impedes our joy. As we co-labor with Father, Son, and Holy Spirit, we will gain confidence in the Father's love. Knowing His great love allows us to stand unwavering in that resolve of His forgiveness. We can tuck His stalwart promise into our belt of truth girded around our loins and become fierce lions for God's Kingdom.

Let's look further and see how joy could have been buried during conception, covered by the wreckage of lies.

My Being Unites In Reverence

Studies show that trauma can start in the womb. Guilt, shame, stress, and toxic emotional trauma can (and often does) compute into the genetic makeup of the growing fetus. Without any resistance, emotionally traumatic experiences are transmitted to the fetus and coded into the very fibers of their being.

The study goes on to say that attached to the umbilical cord, a fetus receives air, food, water, and anything else the mother digests. In addition, the extremely sensitive fetus picks up on the mother's emotion, her internal and external environment, from arguments to verbal stress or emotional stress, chaos in the home environment, and neglect, to name a few (theguesthouseocala.com).

Thank God for reversing every curse that could have been transmitted or coded in every fiber of our being by the enemy, overriding and reprogramming it back to its original, God-designed DNA. My acronym for DNA is "Defeated Never Again." When read backward, it spells AND, so I like to add that we are under

You are healed in His everlasting arms.

the blood of Jesus. So, defeated never again *and* covered in His blood. (My husband is the king of acronyms; I hope to make him proud.)

King David gives our hearts a beautiful prayer of faith in Psalms 86:11 (TLB): "Tell me where you want me to go and I will go there. May every fiber of my being unite in reverence to your name." You are safe and healed within His everlasting arms where you can find refuge with every fiber of your being.

Past Sins, Future Forgiveness

On a side note, as I ponder this fetus article, I'm aware that even my own children were affected by my brokenness – not only outside of the womb, but inside as well. Reflecting on my past shortcomings, I have repented to God and my children and will continue to do so if the Lord recalls a memory that needs addressing.

Even now, as grown men, if I have somehow unknowingly hurt them, I want to make it right to the best of my ability. Saying you're sorry goes a long way. You cannot go wrong if you humbly ask for forgiveness when needed. Be able to forgive yourself as well. I have beat myself up for the hurt I've caused. It is time to release that too, for if you have given it to God, it has been erased.

Even our best, well-meaning intentions to be great parents can fail. I can relate to the saying, "Once upon a time, I was a perfect parent. Then I had children. The End."

Psalm 51:5 (KJV) tells us clearly, "Behold I was shapen in iniquity; and in sin my mother conceived me." Every parent fails from time to time, for we are imperfect human beings. Some walk in more brokenness than others, yet all of us need to forgive and, by God's grace, be forgiven. To walk in wholeness and freedom, it is important to release our parents from any unforgiveness being held against them in regard to how they raised us. In turn, we have to forgive ourselves for blowing it as parents.

Forgiveness is not to be a family affair only, for it holds true for anyone held in our prison of unforgiveness, whether it be a friend, coworker, or a random stranger who has wronged us. Wherever forgiveness, bitterness, and resentment have taken root, they need to be uprooted and eradicated. We will learn more about forgiveness and bitterness in Chapter 10.

John Henry Jowett puts it beautifully in his book *My Daily Meditation for the Circling Year*: "Sin that is unconfessed shuts out the energies of grace. Confession makes the soul receptive to the bountiful waters of life. We open the door to God as soon as we name our sin. Guilt that is penitently confessed is already in the 'consuming fire' of God's love. When I 'acknowledge my sin,' I begin to enter the knowledge of 'pardon, joy, and peace.' But if I hide my sin, I also hide myself from the unsearchable."

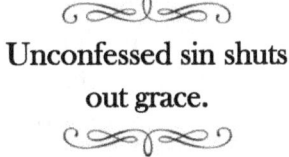

Unconfessed sin shuts out grace.

Those words make me think of one particular episode of the *Gold Rush White Water* TV show my husband and I were watching one night. This show follows a man and his son, along with a team of divers, mountaineers, and bush mechanics, as they explore the white-water rapids of McKinley Creek in Alaska. In search of gold, the series shows them diving deep in raging torrents with a suction dredge. Every episode has peril, disappointment, and joyful celebrations of victory as they stare in awe at shimmering gold flakes and nuggets showing up in the sluice.

This episode was not an exception; it highlighted a greenhorn diver underwater using the hose to comb the floor of the river for gold. Unfortunately, due to his lack of experience, he was sucking up larger rocks that should have been removed by hand, and this clogged the tube, stopping the flow of water, and ultimately gold, from making its way to the top. Eventually, the diver was brought to the surface so a trained teammate could teach him the proper way to vacuum the floor. So, too, can our lives get clogged up with our sin of unrepentance or unforgiveness, blocking the flow of the rich nugget of God's grace, freedom, and joy. Once freed, the blockage becomes a swirl of breakthrough with a fresh anointing of the Holy Spirit.

Excavating Joy

Also, this is key: let the Holy Spirit do the digging. You are not digging up dead-and-buried stuff, it was alive when it was thrown into the grave; shoveling mounds of denial on top just silenced the pain. Repressed memories of traumatic events can be stored, hidden in our unconscious minds. Recall the many times you never picked up the shovel to unearth the hurt; your brain did it for you.

Welcome the gentleness of the Holy Spirit to reveal the pain so it gets healed in a proper and timely manner like the ever-so-delicate touch of an archaeologist. An archaeologist digs carefully in an unhurried rhythm, meticulously brushing away the dirt to expose the treasure beneath. Our true God-given identity got buried under a rubble of lies. Although some liken this process to layers of onions that get peeled off slowly, I prefer my friend Lynn's description about deep-sea diving. The awe, wonder, and beauty of the ocean is revealed at every twist and turn as we dive deeper into His boundless love. Roaring deep calls to roaring deep, or as the The Passion Translation says, "My deep need calls to the deep kindness of your love."

Clemson football coach Dabo Swinney shared his take on Psalm 42:7: "In essence, this is the Spirit of God reaching deep into the spirit of His children, bypassing all that which would attempt to impede that sweet communion and fellowship God so passionately desire to have with us" (Bradenton.com, Article Faith Matters).

God wants our hearts to dive into the ocean of His love and uncover hidden treasures from any areas of the wreckage of brokenness beneath the surface. On our expedition to joy, take your cue from standard diving procedures: use a guideline that aids in visibility, increases confidence, and navigates a diver to safety. We have resources available to us, such as the plumb line of God's Word, the Holy Spirit, strong faith-filled churches, mentors, faith-filled friends, great books that touch on our needs, not to mention godly counselors to help speak into our lives. All these can guide us through murky and uncharted waters. In Isaiah 9:6 (AMPC), God's Word also reminds us, "For to us a Child is born, to us a Son is given; and the government shall be upon His shoulder, and His name shall be called Wonderful Counselor, Mighty God, Everlasting Father [of Eternity], Prince of Peace."

I relied on this verse many times in my life, especially when I could not afford to pay for a counselor. He is faithful, for He is the same Jesus who fed the multitude with only five loaves of bread and two fish. He can most certainly feed your hungry soul. I don't know where I would have been without all the resources God brought to me to find freedom. If you lack in any of those options, ask Father God for all you need, for those who trust in Him lack no good thing.

God always reveals in order to heal, so if He is speaking to you in an area, it is to bring back freedom and reclaim the joy you were robbed of. Have you heard of *naval gazing*? That is us trying to look back, with our own effort and will power, and do something about our past. Instead, turn your heart toward God for the answers while spending time with Him, soaking in His presence in stillness. Gently, He will skim off the dross of impurities that rise to the surface. His love and life-giving water are for you.

"For just one day of intimacy with you is like a thousand days of joy rolled into one! I'd rather stand at the threshold in front of the Gate Beautiful, ready to go in and worship my God, than to live my life without you in the most beautiful palace of the wicked" (Psalm 84:10, TPT).

God Hovers Over Our Emptiness

Even with all the magnificent truth of God's Word and the illustrious science that backs up His creation, our minds can still question our worth in our brokenness. Shame, clinging like a too-tight garment, trauma pinching like shoes too small. We're capable of being ill-fitted right from our conception. Our lives can fall prey to the world's sin-laden state as it spins on its axis 365 times a year. Meant to be an instrument for good, God's invaluable gift to mankind (bestowing free will to all) has sadly, at times, been wielded as a destructive weapon against one another. I, too, have made wrong choices, forging a sword that wounds instead of beating that sword into a plowshare of love. We long for God's healing balm for our injuries, whether self-inflicted or otherwise. We struggle to experience the richness of God's love, because it seems hidden in plain view.

For years, I have wrestled like a UFC fighter, swinging at the enemy to knock out the rapid succession of lies that were hitting me hard and fast. I have spiritual cauliflower ears to prove it. Hungry to be free from the relentless, wearisome battle, I desired with all that was left within me to pin down the big lies clutching my spirit and bring them crashing down to the mat once and for all. To be completely successful in this endeavor, I realize how importance it is to tag-team with Father, Son, and Holy Spirit, forging ahead in a new level of freedom for myself and hopefully others as well. For ultimately, God is the one fighting our battles.

"The Lord will fight for you" (Exodus 14:14 AMPC).

In our journey, we are able to glean victory songs from others. We fight arm in arm for more wholeness, deliverance, and against anything that impedes or distorts the 20/20 vision of our gracious, loving Heavenly Father. While doing this, we sink our heels into the healing mat to claim divine healing in its full capacity, knowing the enemy can't take us down again.

Winning a war is also done in rest and stillness, for that is a powerful, often overlooked form of warfare. The battle belongs to the Lord. "Strength arises as we wait upon the Lord" (Isaiah 40:31). For He lovingly reminds us in Psalm 46:10 (NIV), "Be still and know that I am God." At times it might be difficult waiting for marching orders in the stillness, yet it proves just as crucial as combat.

"I am standing in absolute stillness, silent before the One I love, waiting as long as it takes for Him to rescue me. Only God is my Savior, and He will not fail me" (Psalm 62:5, TPT).

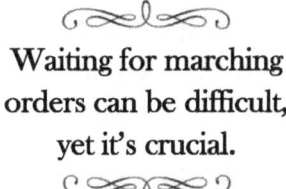

Waiting for marching orders can be difficult, yet it's crucial.

Broods Over Creation

Genesis Chapter 1 gives us a front-row seat to the beginning of creation. Let's peer into the scene.

"In the beginning God (prepared, formed, fashioned, and) created the heavens and the earth. The earth was without form and an empty waste, and darkness was upon the face of the very great deep. The Spirit of God was moving (hovering, brooding) over the face of the waters. And God said, 'Let there be light'; and there was light. And God saw that the light was good (suitable, pleasant) *and* He approved it; and God separated the light from the darkness. And God called the light Day, and the darkness He called Night. And there was evening and there was morning, one day" (Genesis 1:1-5 AMPC).

"The spirit of God brooded over the deep to produce Life" (Living Streams Ministry, www.minstrysamples.com). The Hebrew meaning of brooded or hovered is when a mother bird broods over her eggs to bring forth life (paraphrased). The formless void and emptiness deeply stirred God to speak life and light into the waste and darkness. God was very present at your conception, hovering over the empty and dark areas of your life, eager to fill any gaping wounds devoid of love, joy, and hope with a love that radically transforms us. His tender compassion, grace, and power are still readily available to heal our past and present wounds. That spark of light at your conception will shine even brighter for all to see as you walk in healing from your past trauma into total forgiveness. That divine spark is now a lamp shining brightly, no longer encumbered by a bushel of shame or womb trauma.

"The spirit of God breathed into man is like a living lamp, a shining light searching into the innermost chamber of our being" (Proverbs 20:27 TPT).

"Your lives light up the world. Let others see your light from a distance, for how can you hide a city that stands on a hilltop? And who would light a lamp and then hide it in an obscure place? Instead, it's placed where everyone in the house can benefit from its light. So don't hide your light! Let it shine brightly before others, so that the commendable things you do will shine as light upon them, and then they will give their praise to your Father in heaven" (Matthew 5:14-16, TPT).

The God Of Wonders Is On Your Side

"Never doubt God's mighty power to work in you and accomplish all this. He will achieve infinitely more than your greatest request, your most unbelievable dream, and exceed your wildest imagination! He will outdo them all, for his miraculous power constantly energizes you." (Ephesians 3:20, TPT). Remember this verse. I'm going to talk about it in a moment.

Remember the song "Pure Imagination" from the *Willy Wonka* movie? My heart swells with joy at God's wildest imaginations for us. And you won't even get stuck in the pipe like Augustus Gloop. Ever!

Deconstruct To Reconstruct

Since we are on the topic of wildest imagination and *Willy Wonka & the Chocolate Factory*, I want to share how the mighty power of God pulled a crazy Ephesians 3:20 on me while writing this book. At one point, I thought my manuscript was done. As I headed to what I thought was the home stretch, I heard the Lord say "deconstruct to reconstruct." As I pondered those words in regard to my book, it was confirmed during the writing retreat at Tetelestai Ministries days later.

Indeed, it needed reconstruction. Returning home, I rolled up my sleeves to what felt like a daunting task. With the Lord's help, I completed my reconstruction and was eager to send it to a dear friend to look it over. To my shock, I realized I had reconstructed my whole book from an unedited copy of it. Devastated at this revelation, my emotions ranged from mad to sad as tears welled in my eyes. The task seemed insurmountable. That night, I stepped away from the project as doubts flooded my mind. I wondered if I was even called to write my story. My husband and dear friends prayed for me, and the next morning, I heard the Lord say, "Lay it fallow and step into the hallowed." That sounded good to me, for I was heading to Estes Park in Colorado the next day for a Her Voice rally, and I knew time away would do me good.

Violet, You're Turning Violet

The rally was life-changing, as it always is, and I not only stepped on holy ground, but I also lay my full body down on it. Normally, that is not how I posture myself at a rally, but the Lord was getting my attention, and it was through pain. C.S. Lewis has a beautiful reminder of this. He said, "Pain insists upon being attended to. God whispers to us in our pleasures, speaks in our consciences, but shouts in our pains. It is his megaphone to rouse a deaf world." And let me tell you, I was in pain.

It was not about my book; my stomach was bloating like Violet's when she grabbed Willy Wonka's everlasting gobstopper, popping the gum into her mouth and chomping away. From tomato soup to roast beef, baked potato and finally blueberry pie and creme, it immediately made her bloat up like a giant blueberry. That was exactly how I felt. I'm usually quite fond of dessert.

The Rose Is Red, The Violet, Blue

As I prayed for my stomach earlier that day, the Lord reminded me of being three years old and having bad stomach aches that would wake me up at night, which I believe were attributed to sexual abuse. I was beginning to see He was revealing something that needed healing.

Later that afternoon, during his teaching, Danny McDaniels shared from his book *Freedom: Winning the Battle Within*. He walked us through a group deliverance prayer. Those prayers would forever change me even more than the last time in July 2021 at the Her Voice rally at Camp Crestview in Corbett, Oregon. As he began to call out sexual abuse, incest, molestation, and rape, I moved myself to the upper level of the auditorium to lay my bloated stomach on the ground. I was in so much pain and fear of embarrassing myself with so much trapped gas. Before we prayed, he told us that we might cough, cry, yawn, or have a runny nose because the demonic oppression comes out through the openings in our body. I never heard him say anything about gas, and believe me, I would have much preferred a yawn as their way of escape.

As I positioned myself on the ground, I checked my phone and saw a message from my dear friend Debbie; that was straight from heaven. It read, "Just a quick word from the Lord. Get up close, daughter; get up real close. I have something for you. Something special that you are not expecting. I love you with undying love. I have known you before you were placed in your mother's womb. Fearfully and wonderfully created by My own hands. But you do need to come closer. Empty yourself and humble yourself. Get ready for My Word to touch your life as I have said. Even your socks will be blessed off, says your Lord." It made me giggle; it was as if she knew one way or the other that I might be emptying myself that night.

God loves you with undying love and created you with His own hands.

"Your will, not mine, Lord Jesus," I said to myself. And so, I got closer, humbled and emptied myself with the help of beautiful people not only praying for me at home but also in Colorado. Precious women like Sophie, Jessica, and Brenda had my back in prayer with love and compassion. This created a safe environment for me to cry from the depth of pain that a little girl and teenager had been, letting things come up and out for good. It was the most free I have ever felt in 60 years.

And whenever I remember that the Lord met me as I lay on the carpet in Colorado, bloated up like a blueberry, it reminds me that author and pastor Jenny Donnelly is definitely right: "Dignity is highly overrated" (from her book, *Wake Up Dead*).

Hallowed Ground

When I returned home on Saturday evening, my stomach felt the best it had felt in a very long time. I woke up on Sunday around 5:00 a.m. to a peaceful prompting from the Lord to research Freemason ritual abuse. Before I go any further, I want to make one thing clear: not all Freemasons are involved in such atrocities. I also believe in forgiveness for all injustices we suffer. Jesus Christ has forgiven us; so, too, we must forgive others. It's not easy by any means, but necessary and so utterly liberating.

As I read some articles that morning, nothing jumped out at me; it didn't seem like any of those things had ever happened to me. I asked my husband to pray for me, and it was then when images flooded my mind, which led to a couple of hours of newly revealed details, puzzle pieces coming together, and a realization that some things *had* happened to me as a child, which my mind could not handle. Also that day, another key player in my abuse was confirmed...someone I never could have believed.

Thirteen years ago, the Lord revealed my dad's sexual abuse to me through someone, which I will talk about later in the book. However, on this day, it seemed I could handle more heartbreak because of all the grief being released. I simply followed the Lord's prompts and listened to the directions of the Holy Spirit. Though it was difficult, I felt so free to have finally known more about my past to forgive those who had wronged me in their own brokenness.

Going to church that sunny day, my face glowed so much that people even commented about it. No more dark secrets the enemy could use against me to block the living water that flows out of my belly. And guess what day this truth gem was found? On Halloween! The very day God chose to reverse the curse of all demonic activities that were carried out on me as a child. I now stand on hallowed ground, completely free, writing this book with a depth of freedom as never before. My heart's cry is for you to find your hallowed, holy ground as you journey to freedom and wholeness.

From Our Whys To God's Wonder

Step One: Learn to recognize the profound love God has for you. Train your heart and mind to follow the generous breadcrumbs that lead you to the Bread of Life. Once there, feast on His warm, satisfying love for you that is far greater than sliced bread and butter.

Step Two: Meditate on the Word of God, especially Psalm 139. Let it flood your soul with light and love.

Step Three: Ask the Lord to help you forgive anyone who needs your forgiveness in regard to yourself or others.

Now, be open to allow the Lord to examine you. Let Him see if there is any hidden thing that is encumbering your walk and freedom in Christ, which He died for you to have. Take time to write them down here or in your journal.

_____
_____
_____
_____
_____

*Note: *Reclaimed Joy* has a companion journal available with many of the verses used in the book for easy access.

You have taken courageous steps to a beautiful path of greater peace and joy.

"The Lord God is my Strength, my personal bravery, and my invincible army; He makes my feet like hinds' feet and will make me to walk [not to stand still in terror, but to walk] and make [spiritual] progress upon my high places [of trouble, suffering, or responsibility]!"
—Habakkuk 3:19, AMPC

"Forgive yourself for not knowing what you didn't know before you learned it."
—Maya Angelou

Reclaiming Prayer

Precious Heavenly Father, we thank You for the gift of being fearfully and wonderfully made, and for Your kindness toward us that leads us to repentance. "For you bring me a continual revelation of resurrection life, the path to the bliss that brings me face to face with you" (Psalm 16:11 TPT). We are made whole in Your presence.

Chapter 2

Reclaiming Joy

The Lord Heals You

"You've gone into my future to prepare the way, and in kindness you follow behind me to spare me from the harm of my past."
—Psalm 139:5 (TPT)

Jesus Heals Our Owies

Infancy is the building block of the beginning stages of our lives. It is pivotal that in those developmental times, a sense of being loved, protected, and significant is cultivated. We have intrinsic value from the moment of conception. We are precious human beings; we matter to God and others. Unfortunately, not everybody had that warm welcome into the world.

Some of us may have felt unloved, unwanted, and unimportant. We all have boo-boos from our past. For a few of us, all we need is a little validation, maybe a kiss from Jesus on our owie, and we're good to go. For others, not so much. Our injury impacted us immensely; our hearts have been broken and are still bleeding. No matter if we need a small Band-Aid, industrial-strength gauze bandage, or major surgery, God's got it all. We are covered by His grace and mercy, and that is the best coverage *ever*.

Exit Stage Right

Exiting the womb and entering the world opens up limitless possibilities God richly desires to bestow on us. "His heart is for us to know Him intimately, for He [earnestly] waits [expecting, looking, and longing] to be gracious to you; and therefore He lifts Himself up, that He may have mercy on you and show loving-kindness to you. For the Lord is a God of justice. Blessed (happy, fortunate, to be envied) are all those who [earnestly] wait for Him, who expect and look and long for Him [for His victory, His favor, His love, His peace, His joy, and His matchless, unbroken companionship]" (Isaiah 30:18 AMPC [partially paraphrased]).

In the midst of all this beauty and truth for the taking outside of the womb, the enemy of this world gained more latitude, maneuvering in his bigger playing field called earth. At birth, out of the protection of the womb, we emerge into a whole new world filled with amazing wonders and potentials. We can rest in the comfort of what the Lord promises: "...heaven is My throne and the earth my footstool..." (Isaiah 66:1, AMPC). So, we are good to go, no matter what; God has got our back. However, let's face it, if Satan had a closet full of printed t-shirts, one of his favorites would probably say: Does Not Play Well With Others.

He is the earth's biggest bully and can stir up more *why* questions to fill our minds. Thankfully, we have King Jesus who sends the neighborhood bully running. Psalm 17:6-7 (MSG) expresses it so beautifully: "I call to you, God, because I'm sure of an answer. So—answer! Bend our ear! Listen sharp! Paint grace-graffiti on the fences; take in your frightened children who are running from the neighborhood bullies straight to you."

"I call to you, God, because I'm sure of an answer. So—answer!"

And here is a grace-graffiti verse from Psalms 71:4-8 (TPT): "Let me escape from these cruel and wicked men, and save me from the hands of the evil one. For you are my only hope, Lord! I've hung on to you, trusting in you all my life. It was you who supported me from the day I was born, loving me, helping me through my life's journey. You've made me into a miracle;

no wonder I trust you and praise you forever! Many marvel at my success, but I know it is all because of you, my mighty protector! I'm overflowing with your praise for all you've done, and your splendor thrills me all day long."

The Right Exit

Growing up, Saturday morning cartoons were a highlight of the weekend. Whenever I hear "exit stage left," I think of Hanna Barbera's Snagglepuss, a dapper pink mountain lion dressed in finery who had an affinity to the theater. Snagglepuss was fond of sayings things like, "Heavens to Murgatroyd!" and "Exit stage left!" which were some of his popular catchphrases.

When we exit the womb, we do not exit stage left; we exit stage right and come into the arms of our loving Heavenly Father. He already knows this life will have hardship, loss, and disappointment. Jesus reminded His disciples of it in John 16:33 (TPT): "And everything I've taught you is so that the peace which is in me will be in you and will give you great confidence as you rest in me. For in this unbelieving world you will experience trouble and sorrows, but you must be courageous, for I have conquered the world!"

Heavens to Murgatroyd, how comforting! We are in God's hands right from conception, gestation, through birth, to life, and even unto death. Nothing can separate us from His love. The Bible refers to the right side as a special place of honor and a metaphor for the omnipotence of God. Remember, Psalm 139:10 (TPT) says, "Wherever I go, your hand will guide me, your strength will empower me."

Rest in that, God's beloved children. His soft, gentle, and yet sturdy hands and loving arms will embrace and protect you always, for He promises to keep you forever.

Unbreakable And Inextinguishable

Isaiah 42:3 (AMP) says, "A bruised reed He will not break [off], and a dimly burning wick He will not extinguish [He will not harm those who are weak and suffering]; He will faithfully bring forth justice." Jesus fans the dimly burning wick until the flames roar. He is gentle toward us when we are weakest and makes us strong again with His tender loving care.

I remember on my 11th birthday, I thought for sure my brother Troy was going to get me a dress for my Barbie doll. That, however, never happened. Instead, he thought I would enjoy having birthday candles that did not blow out in what seemed like forever. What 11-year-old girl wouldn't love almost passing out, trying to blow out her cake candles in front of her friends? Happy birthday to me! Apparently, he thought a cute little Barbie dress as my gift was highly overrated.

Now, I see the value of his gift, which still makes me laugh to this day. It is a beautiful reminder of how playful he was throughout his life. God knows the desires of our hearts and just what we need to be all He created us to be. It's like having your birthday cake and eating it too, minus trying to blow out indestructible birthday candles. He wants to turn our dimly burning wick into an unquenchable flame that no amount of boisterous lung capacity can blow out. That, my friend, is a gift so worth getting.

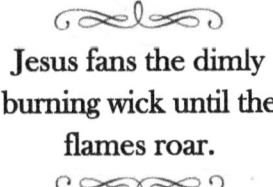

Jesus fans the dimly burning wick until the flames roar.

Bulrushes To Breakthrough

And about that bruised reed, God's Word says, "He will not break off a damaged cattail..." Though He sees our weakness, He will never disregard it. Instead, He sees greatness arising from it. In all of His compassion to deliver us from our broken parts, He will also lovingly expose any hidden areas, bringing complete restoration. Remember, He reveals it to heal it. Just like Moses lay hidden in bulrushes, waiting for deliverance, so, too, do we. We move from the bulrushes of our brokenness to breakthrough as God's redemption glory floats us right into our God-given destiny.

God applauds your baby steps of faith just as much as your big leaps, and He will never grow tired of your *whys*. Your *whys* are the very thing He uses to show you His glory. God is the custom reframer, replacing your hurts with His glory.

God's Custom Reframing

God is longing to reframe and reclaim any heartbreak or disappointment into the proper framework of His redeeming love. Giving you all the necessary tools and resources to do it, His supplies for our wholeness are endless, effective, and lasting. The world, no matter what it offers, cannot do that.

The Lord wants to do this glorious work in any area of our life that needs restoration. He offers us a do-over or, in golf terms, a mulligan - a fresh perspective. Just like the professionals that frame your precious memories, let God reframe your outlook on past hurts. He can reframe your attitude from negativity into pure joy. Countless times, I have bought cheap frames because, well, they were cheap, or I was in a hurry to frame something quickly. Then, the frame or back hook breaks because it could not hold its own weight, wasting time and money, which were the two things I set out not to do.

If we allow ourselves to wait upon the Lord, we not only renew our strength, but we also renew our mind, which is a game-changer. Surrendering to the Lord is crucial for Him to do the necessary work. We might be waiting on God to move in an area, but at times, He is waiting for us to relinquish our free will for His will, which is always picture perfect.

Is God waiting for you to relinquish your free will for His will?

Once snuggled in His will, instead of rushing ahead of Him, we are able to join in lockstep with our transformation. Satan may be in a hurry, but God is not.

Vroom Vroom

My husband and I were in California a while back celebrating our 60th birthdays. When we go to Disneyland, I, without fail, want to be the first in line to the park and the last to leave. I get so amped up. My husband loves teasing me by saying, "Let's hurry up to go have fun!" In reality, what

I do is stressful.

One morning, I was sleeping when I heard audibly, "I love it when you go vroom vroom." And right after that, the sound of a car reviving up its engine on the street next to our hotel room got me fully awake. I asked Kevin, "Did you say 'I love it when you go vroom vroom'?" Though I could never have imagined him saying such a thing, ever. Of course, his answer was "No." I realized it was the Lord's way of telling me that Satan loves it when I go vroom vroom to rev my emotional and physical engines, not walking in a place of peace. It transformed my Disneyland visit, for we never were the first ones there, neither were we the last to leave.

There is nothing wrong with going early and staying late if it is done in peace and unity, but mine rarely was. Obtaining that did not come easily, for I had a deeply ingrained mindset that needed God's help and personal choices to correct.

The amazing thing is, just recently I have been seeing the words *vroom vroom*. So, I said, "Okay, Lord, what else does this mean?" Another meaning is *roar*. How appropriate, for I have been praying for boldness and courage. God is so resourceful. Satan loves nothing more than to rush us and hush us from declaring boldly God's goodness in a posture of peace.

However, when we stay with Jesus as we wait, it fosters a special environment. The weight of anything we are carrying unnecessarily is released, things like guilt, condemnation, false accusations, and lies. Yoked with Jesus every day, our chains break and we will be set free. Our propensity to rush is replaced with His peace. Our inclination to be hushed, silencing our God-given voice, receives His great exchange. That, right there, is one heck of a reason to rev up your spiritual engines and roar.

Wrongful Ownership

At a very young age, I believed I caused my mother's heart palpitations. She got it when she was pregnant, and it lasted until the day she died. I remember her telling me that she was jumping up and down while I was in the womb for fear that her heart was going to stop beating. Each time her heart palpitated, she was afraid of dying.

Unfortunately, this condition was triggered by frequent stress. Doctors believed it was caused by the shock of Brent's death. So, instead of her having a nervous breakdown, it went into her heart. Perhaps that was true, or maybe it was panic attacks she was unable to overcome. Only God knows. I do know that throughout my life, I always tried to make it better. When I was a young child, not only did I feel responsible for her palpitations, but also, each time she got them, I feared I would lose her. She never once said I caused them. I just took that upon myself. It became a vicious cycle of blaming myself and living with intense fear. When I was in my 40s, the fear of her dying from them lessened, and the healing revelation that I did not cause her condition came.

Sadly, we can take ownership of someone's hardship when it is not ours to carry. We can easily drift into others' lanes of accountability, not paying attention to our own. As I mentioned, my mother never once implied that I caused her palpitations, neither did she accuse me of it. We can allow vain imaginations to run amuck in our thinking, and the enemy, who is the accuser of the brethren, sees weak areas of our lives. He seizes the opportunity, grabbing the golden ring.

Flying Horses For The Win

Grabbing the golden ring derives its original meaning from the gold or brass rings hanging on the outside of a carousel. One is expected to reach out and grab ahold of it; in doing so, they receive a free ride. Carousels are a whimsical reminiscence of our childhood. Isn't that just like the enemy, trying to get a free ride and dizzily fleecing us from the joys of childhood? Yet God is the God of harmony, not confusion or instability (I Corinthians 14:33, TPT). We praise You, Lord, for that!

There are still a handful of merry-go-rounds with golden rings today. I'm adding that to my bucket list: riding a flying horse to victory. Neener, neener!

Take that, Satan.

The Dizzying Ride

Though I would rather write about the childhood joys of riding a brightly colored carousel, the truth of the matter is, one of the most painful and dizzying parts of my past has been the multiple-time sexual abuses that have ravished my soul. Beginning at infancy, by a close family member, it opened the door to varying degrees of sexual molestation, including rape in my senior year of high school. I believe even one inappropriate sexual touch is too much. Each violation robs a piece of your innocence, morphing your reality, twisting and touching every area of your life.

When Pastor Ben Rose was sharing his painful journey of overcoming sexual abuse and addiction, he recalled someone saying to him, "Where do you even file that?" How true? Where does a small, pure child file such atrocities at such a tender age? For me, it got repressed, stuffed, denied, or I blamed myself for them until I was 47 years old. Now, with an adult perspective and the proper handling and healing of these files of information, it has been placed in the *round file* or *file 13*, a fancy U.S. Military term for *the trash*. She shoots, she scores, and the crowd goes wild!

It has been a long journey to get to a place of deeper freedom and healing, for many of those memories had been repressed for years. Throughout this book, I will be addressing some issues that manifest themselves from abuse, abandonment, or low self-esteem, with a more in-depth look at my own journey. You can overcome sexual abuse trauma with God's help, and I'll give you basic personal takeaways you can use for a range of hardships and disappointments. You need practical, shoe-leather faith to walk into your freedom.

When we are done, we get the glorious chore of taking out any trash, only keeping our treasured testimony of His faithfulness.

Take Out The Trash

"Yes, furthermore, I count everything as loss compared to the possession of the priceless privilege (the overwhelming preciousness, the surpassing worth, and supreme advantage) of knowing Christ Jesus my Lord and of progressively becoming more deeply and intimately acquainted with Him [of perceiving and recognizing and understanding Him more fully and clearly]. For His sake I have lost everything and consider it all to be mere rubbish (refuse, dregs), in order that I may win (gain) Christ (the Anointed One)" (Philippians 3:8, AMPC).

Paul said that he counted everything as loss; even his accomplishments became a mere pile of manure in comparison to the delightfulness of knowing Christ. If only we could gladly chuck our accomplishments in exchange for the joy of knowing Him more fully. So, too, let's take the lies, abuse, and any hardship that weighed us down to the trash heap, carrying only the weight of His glory back in with us.

"I don't depend on my own strength to accomplish this; however I do have one compelling focus: I forget all of the past as I fasten my heart to the future instead" (Philippians 3:13-14, TPT).

Take the lies, abuse, and hardships to the trash, and carry only His glory back.

From Our *Whys* To God's Wonders

Restore For More

What owie did God heal this week or month?

_____
_____
_____

How did that healing bring you closer to Him?

_____
_____
_____

Is there any hardship or area in your life that you have taken ownership of, but God wants you to release today?

_____
_____
_____

"God often digs wells of joy with spades of sorrow." —Anonymous

"It's never too late to have a happy childhood." —Berkeley Breathed

Reclaiming Prayer

Thank You, Jesus, that You are so worthy of our praise. Your love breaks every chain that has held us in captivity. We press into You for Your image and not that of the world. We rejoice that Your love is better than life itself, and You long to heal our owies into wholeness.

Chapter 3

Whoville

The Lord Hears You

"It's impossible to disappear from you or to ask the darkness to hide me, for your presence is everywhere, bringing light into my night."
—Psalm 139:11 (TPT)

He Hears Your Cry

In Dr. Seuss' book, *Horton Hears a Who*, you will find Horton the elephant splashing in a pool, until he realizes a speck of dust is talking to him. The whole town of Whoville lived precariously on an itsy-bitsy speck of dust. Talk about tiny homes. The town, a mere dot, was on the brink of destruction – a flimsy piece of dust floating in the wind, aimlessly caught in its mercy, until that one splendid day Horton heard its faint cry. He vowed to protect it from then on, giving them value and honor, declaring, "A person is a person, no matter how small."

How much more does our Heavenly Father do this for us? Let's revisit Isaiah 42:3 with a new lens from The Message translation:

"He won't brush aside the bruised and the hurt and he won't disregard the small and insignificant, but he'll steadily and firmly set things right. He won't tire out and quit. He won't be stopped until he's finished his work—to set things right on earth..."

You may be struggling with your self-worth, identity, depression, or fear somewhere A lie has dislodged you from your God-given destiny. That is right where Satan wants you: floating around, drifting further from the truth and your God-given calling. We have a loving Heavenly Father who is far more faithful than Horton when it comes to rescuing us.

For He is "our Comforter, Counselor, Helper, Intercessor, Advocate, Strengthener, Standby, and the giver of eternal salvation. He will not only teach us all things that bring us to victory, but He will carry us if need be" (John 14:26, paraphrased, AMPC). Cry out to God; press in to seek peace and pursue, and you will reap the benefits of experiencing a breakthrough. You matter. Not only do you matter, but you also have a powerful voice for God's Kingdom that will ignite a flame in others. Being able to speak life-giving words of comfort protects the broken and hurting. Your life-giving words hold them up with respect, love, and honor, loving them just as you have been so profoundly loved by God and others.

> **You matter, and you have a powerful voice.**

Our Sacred Stories

Our lives, like diaries, can be very personal. Some parts of our lives, we may never want to share with everyone, and that is okay as long as you have at least one safe person to share it with. Share it with a safe person so it no longer causes you to walk in sin or unresolved shame. We are forgiven, cleansed, and washed in the blood. "As far as the east is from the west, so far has He removed our transgressions from us" (Psalm 103:12, AMPC).

Let the Holy Spirit lead to you a safe person for you to share with. James tells us in Chapter 5 verse 16 (AMPC) to "Confess to one another your faults (your slips, your false steps, your offenses, your sins) and pray for one another, that you may be healed and restored (to a spiritual tone of mind and heart).

A Simple Hello

My friendship with Michelle was birthed with my one act of obedience and flourished with her countless ones. We met when I worked at Christian Supply in the gift department. As I busily stocked greeting cards like a ninja, Michelle, a store regular, was busy picking out cards to bless people. Yes, of course she was. The Lord gently nudged me to talk to her. Being the work horse I was, I began shooing away those thoughts like horse flies on a hot summer day. *Too busy* was my motto. Finally, I succumbed to the still small voice that was impervious to my *la la la la I cannot hear you* approach. That small act of obedience led to a 30-year friendship, and she has poured into my life a tangible picture of God's love and joy since day one. My heart bursts with gratitude.

Funny thing is, she wanted to talk to me that day too, but thought I had it all together (ROTFL)! It is so easy to judge a book by its cover – our human nature excels at it. First page into this book (me) though, she saw how hurting and broken I was. No amount of makeup, quaffed hair or cute little outfit could hide it for long. Her love and commitment to me became a soothing sound of safety, lulling me out from underneath the heavy rock of shame that my soul languished under. Excavated up from the heap of lies, God brought me out into His glorious light, all because I said yes to Him and yes to those He brought into my life for my healing. To think it started with a simple hello...

Say Hello To Obedience

Listen for your loving Heavenly Father to guide you when the spiritual light is red to stop and/or green to go.

Unpacking The Suitcase

To be honest, it has been a long, painful journey of unpacking all the sexual abuse I had encountered. Each person, each act of that person's brokenness, in turn, broke me. That impact took parts of me that the Lord has and continues to restore.

My sexual abuses were a mixture of completely buried encounters, some too deep to recognize the destructive root system that produced bad fruit entrenching my soul with its lies. The bulk of the sexual abuses fell into the category of *it was my fault*, and their lack of severity, by comparison, felt as though it wasn't really a form of "abuse" at all. Therefore, this category of abuses fell into mishandled files that could not get the needed attention to heal properly.

Sexual abuse isn't the only thing that can get us off track. Other wounds can heighten the appeal of our fleshly nature to soothe the pain in unhealthy ways, overriding the things of God and the Holy Spirit. Instead, we yield to the temptations that only bring a false sense of comfort, consuming falsehoods and misconceptions our Heavenly Father never meant for us to digest.

It's like the time I sent off a fresh batch of homemade dog cookies to celebrate our dog Scooby's birthday. I joyfully handed it to our boys' neighborhood friends, instructing them that it was for their dog, Cheyenne, to celebrate Scooby's special day. The things you do as a home school mom! However, they somehow forgot to tell their father, and he thought the treats were safe for human consumption. Therefore, he consumed something he was not meant to. When he thanked me for the yummy cookies, I sheepishly had to tell him they were actually for their dog.

The point is, we cannot keep consuming things that were not meant for our consumption. What we keep spiritually digesting and confessing with our mouths eventually catches up with us. Perhaps if he'd eaten those dog cookies every day, our neighbor would have started scratching rapidly behind his ears, his hands cupped in a paw-like fashion...one never knows. That familiar saying "You are what you eat" and what we confess with our mouths can be for good or for harm. May the Lord open our eyes and heart to whatever lies we are digesting, whether consciously or unconsciously. May they all be uprooted completely, helping us to be overcomers, no longer operating through misguided words or deeds.

"Your words were found, and I ate them; and Your words were to me a joy and the rejoicing of my heart, for I am called by Your name, O Lord God of hosts" (Jeremiah 15:16 (AMPC).

So much tastier than a dog biscuit.

Excavating The Lies

It was habitually quite vague; I could not put my finger on it or call it as it were, but it went on for years. It was not until I turned 40 when the dam of pent-up emotions sprung a sizable leak. Intense emotional and even different physical pains took their toll until the dam fully broke seven years later. The chipping away was not only God, but also by the love of my husband, precious mentors and friends, navigating me to safety from the choppy waters of unresolved trauma. My husband showed me love and understanding even when he did not know the depths of my abuse. How could he? I did not even know its severity. Then, came my precious mentors like Michelle who poured love and wisdom over my bleeding heart like a balm.

One day, my mentor Lynn asked me a gentle, loving question while we were talking on the phone. She simply asked, "Could you possibly have been abused?" I cannot say what it was, but her tender approach and question made me feel heard, like Whoville being ever so gently placed upon a clover with Horton's promise of protection.

That beautiful woman made it her commitment to take me under her wing; she walked me through it for seven years until I had glorious freedom. Not only was she there the day I was profoundly set free and miraculously delivered, she still cheers me on to this day with her love and unwavering friendship as does my mentor Michelle

The Miracle Ball

In the days leading up to being 47 years old, the crescendo of revelation was filled with lots of twists and turns. It all started with the Miracle Ball, or I should say it got the ball rolling to propel me into my healing. My lower back and tailbone were hurting, so I thought I would use the Miracle Ball method: a small ball you roll back and forth to relieve pain. It had worked for Kevin's back splendidly, so why not? I loved it so much so I probably overdid it. Can we say obsessive-compulsive behavior? That was me before I was healed. Actually, it was a cleverly disguised way to get me to the doctor, which worked swimmingly.

Spoiler alert **TMI** follows in the next paragraph, so you might want to skip ahead if you get easily offended by too much information. And believe me, I have asked the Lord why this had to be a pivotal part of my testimony. It was a truly humbling experience I'd prefer not to talk about. But now, looking back, it is rather humorous.

How I Spent My Summer Vacation

So, drum roll, please. Rolling on the ball excessively led to severe hemorrhoids. Who knew? Some miracle, huh? I would jokingly say if I had to write a paper on how I spent my summer vacation, it would have been captioned: "I Spent My Summer at Sandy Hemorrhoid Clinic." It's the one on the busy street with a big circular fishbowl window for easy inside viewing.

It was not only the discomfort, something was being triggered deep within my spirit that was perplexing. There was far too much angst over the ailment. Though I pleaded through the ugly cries and tears for the Lord to heal me, I saw no manifestation.

Waiting for my healing answer, from time to time, I walked around our house or backyard, wearing a tiara, claiming I was a daughter of the King. It was tangible and had a touch of whimsy (and I like both), yet I still found myself at the famous clinic. It was so famous, it once boasted a map with a bazillion brightly colored pins representing all the people who traveled to it for healing. Yay me! I made the club. For those with inquiring minds, I did not wear my tiara to the hemorrhoid clinic. I did not want to be the butt of anyone's jokes.

Everything Is Just Ducky

On my trek to the barren desert of appointments, I bought a couple of rubber duckies to line the dashboard to remind me that everything was going to be just ducky. Their cheery faces greeted me after each treatment.

With that behind me (pun intended), I was still in turmoil, as memories of abuse slowly surfaced and I could no longer excuse them away or push them under. The memories were indeed painful to look at, and yet a necessary part of my healing. In that intense pain of dealing with my past, I was becoming aware that I was not responsible. It was not my fault. The lies were excavated and brought to light from the dungeon of my repressed memories. The musty lid was lifted, releasing its contents for God's healing breath to blow new life in the once-cramped and dank quarters.

One day, during my final treatments, the Lord brought Psalm 51:6 to my mind: "Behold You desire truth in the inner being: make me therefore to know wisdom in my inmost heart" (AMPC). I said, "Lord, what truth do I not know about? I want to know anything that is hidden from me so I can be free."

The memories were painful to look at, but a necessary part of my healing.

Days later, I was in such a deep funk and smelled funky too, for I was so depressed I could not even shower. Moping around in a depressing fog, I reached for the water jug in the refrigerator. I got a whiff of a smell. It triggered a memory that made me have the deepest grief of my abuse journey thus far. The thought of it made my knees buckle; I felt a swift, powerful punch to my gut. Tears started to flow. "No, God, it cannot be." For it was someone I loved dearly and had trusted my whole life. It was my father. It was like a horrible nightmare I wanted so desperately to wake up from, yet knowing that the sinking feeling I was drowning in was my new reality, and I needed a lifeline to swim to safety.

Numb, I tried to call my mentor Lynn, but could not get ahold of her. Still restless, I got on our computer and saw an email from my friend Susy, who happens to be Lynn's sister-in-law. She had sent an email inviting me to come over to her home. In my despondency, I had lost track of the days and thought I had missed it. When I called Susy to tell her how sorry I was, she said, "No, it is today, Lisa. And Lynn and Mercedes are here now." Mercedes was visiting from Argentina where Joe and Susy had moved back to the States from two years earlier.

Mercedes had been miraculously healed from Multiple Sclerosis at a Benny Hinn rally, for she went in wheelchair-bound and walked out, wheelchair-free. Who would not like to visit with a woman who experienced such glorious healing? She also had given me a word the last time she visited the States. In Spanish, she said, "You have the key to your healing." I did not get it at the time even after Susy translated it. It was not until that phenomenal day of deliverance when I grabbed ahold of the golden key to freedom, becoming thoroughly aware of its liberation.

Showered And Shining

People might say, "Let me jump in the shower real quick," and I did my jump like the Energizer Bunny on steroids. Hair still wet, I raced to my car to get to Susy's house only a couple of blocks away. Stepping into her home, I stood with not only wet hair but a pale-yellow face that looked like I had just seen a ghost. Here, greeting me, was my mentor Lynn, who I tried to call, along with Mercedes and Susy. Like cheery duckies standing all in a row, it reminded me everything would be just ducky.

> "Openness is to wholeness as secrets are to sickness."

I plopped on the sofa and began to tell them my very fresh revelation. They immediately surrounded me with prayer, and I sobbed like never before. Words spoken over me through these precious women were direct downloads from God, undeniably confirming that my fears about my dad were true. For all this to have come together, it was absolutely miraculous. You cannot tell me there is no God. His handprint is all over our lives. I have evidence of that undeniable fact. His timing was perfect. The events were supernatural, and I'm overwhelmingly grateful; God cares so much for each one of us that He goes to great lengths to get us healed. It is simply mind-blowing. What is even more mind blowing is on that same day, Mercedes gave me a detailed description of another abuser in my life with pinpoint accuracy. It took me 13 years and a trip to Colorado for the Her Voice Rally to get this full revelation to overcome it (with God's help). Barbara Johnson once wrote, "Openness is to wholeness as secrets are to sickness." We are not always aware of all the secrets we carry; however, God knows precisely how to draw them out lovingly and graciously. Those beautiful prayers that day were spoken over me in Spanish, English, and tongues, reviving my spirit without fully understanding it all. Touching the deepest parts of my being, they healed cavernous wounds. One thing that came through loud and clear was how I was loved by God passionately and loved by beautiful women who loved God with a passion.

My heart was incredibly light and profoundly free as I left that day. Getting into my car, I checked to see how puffy my eyes were after my boatload of tears. Tilting the rear-view mirror, sho'nuff, puffy eyes peered back at me as expected. But there was something new. It was as if God took a squeegee to wash away the dull lifelessness that had pooled in them. Eyes that had seen too much and carried a secret far too long were now sparkling and twinkly. Not only did God fill me up with the spirit of liberty, but I also got squeaky clean eyes that now reflected the true window of my soul just as Jesus Christ intended.

"But the moment one turns to the Lord with an open heart, the veil is lifted and they see. Now, the 'Lord' I'm referring to is the Holy Spirit, and wherever he is Lord, there is freedom" (2 Corinthians 3:16-17 TPT).

The Lord did not drop the ball in regard to my healing, neither has He with yours. He will allow your path to wind through the love of family and friends, then you will come out stronger than when you first surveyed the seemingly ominous blocked trail to freedom. Those heaping mounds of sorrow now gone, our joy is unearthed and our path clear once and for all. It makes me want to say, "Supercalifragilisticexpialidocious," and shout, "Hallelujah!"

Supercalifragilisticexpialidocious

The word Supercalifragilisticexpialidocious came from the Sherman brothers in the 1964 movie *Mary Poppins*. Apparently, it was the perfect song for her to sing while in a scene that had her at a loss for words. Though there seemed to be conflicting stories as to how the brothers came up with the word. One story claimed they double-talked words to each other as children. The meaning is as follows:

Super – Above
Cali – Beauty
Fragilistic – Delicate
Expiali – To atone
Docious – Educable

The above translates as *atoning for educability through delicate beauty* (Wikipedia).

When you dig deeper and look at atonement, it's *an effort to make up for wrongdoing so you can be in harmony* (Vocabulary.com/Dictionary).

In other words, to atone means to *make amends to repair a wrong done, to remove the guilt of man,* and that is just what Jesus did.

"He is the atoning sacrifice for our sins, and not only ours but also the sins of the whole world" (1 John 2:2, TPT). We all need atonement; some may even need it super-sized like me. No need to say a big, long, fancy word to ask Jesus into your heart and for the forgiveness of your sins. He waits with great anticipation to welcome you with open arms and your humble prayers. Have you walked a path of brokenness? Let God bring you comfort, as only He truly can.

From Our *Whys* To The God Of Wonder

Here are a few ideas that helped me overcome the trauma of my sexual abuse and other areas of my life too. These are one-size-fits-all. And before you look at the list, remember life is an ongoing expedition, even without abuse. We never arrive until we arrive in heaven. There is no shame in your pilgrimage or testimony. God delights in each step you take. Even if you fall, He will get you back on your feet and cheer you on all the way to the finish line, just like any doting father would.

You Time

1. Learn to love yourself. Take time to do something for yourself. A warm bath, read a good book, a lovely walk, whatever makes your heart happy. It does not have to involve spending much (or any) money.

2. Become childlike. There is a big difference between being childish and becoming childlike. God longs for you to enjoy the moment. Blow some bubbles, take delight in the childlike wonderment of a ladybug, a flower with dew drops. After the revelation of my abuse, I took baths with rubber duckies and lots of bubbles. I reclaimed my stolen childhood with the weapon of childlike joy. Don't be ashamed of doing what heals your heart with the prompting of the Holy Spirit.

"Learn this well: unless you receive the revelation of the kingdom the same was a little child receives it, you will never be able to enter in" (Luke 18:17, TPT).

3. Keep a journal. Write your thoughts, prayers, favorite Bible verses, hopes, and dreams. Pour your heart out to your Papa Daddy. Let God place a healing salve over areas that hurt so deeply. By the way, calling God *Papa Daddy* did not happen for me until this year, so don't feel bad if that saying makes you uncomfortable. It once did for me too. Earthly father wounds can run deep, and only your Heavenly Father can truly heal them to their core. I will share more about the importance of journaling in Chapter 10.

4. Read the Word. Store it in your heart; speak it out loud; use it as a prayer. "Your word have I laid up in my heart that I might not sin against you" (Psalm 119:11, AMPC).

5. Find safe people who you can share with. Having safe, nontoxic people in your life who you can share hard things with is so important. You do not have to share or confess everything unless you feel a strong prompting from the Lord. There is great value in confessing our sins to safe, godly people who will regard your pearls of suffering with great care as I mentioned earlier. My friend Lynn also shared with me a litmus test of sorts. She asked, "Would you be comfortable naked in front of that person?" It was an intense question, but it made me think, *Who do I want my soul to be naked before?* Coming from a girl with such modesty, I told the gym teacher that I had my period every gym day so I would not have to shower in front of the other girls. I took Lynn's hypothetical question very seriously.

Obviously, there will come a time when your wounds will no longer be gaping or tender to the touch as they once were. Now, a protective scar shows where healing took place, no longer able to get infected with people's opinions of you. Satan wants us to keep everything inside for fear of being unlovable, whispering, "If they knew that about you, they would not like you." Speaking it out loud to safe people will bring it to the light of love and acceptance. Dispelling the darkness with each confession, weakening the enemy's grasp, until it becomes a distant memory, permanently released from the mocking grip of shame.

I grab ahold of Your hand and truths, for Your Word tells us You're not a man that You should lie. Thank You for setting me free, and those who are set free are free indeed.

"God is not a man, that He should tell or act in a lie, neither the son of man, that He should feel repentance or compunction [for what He has promised]. Has He said and shall He not do it? Or has He spoken and shall He not make it good?" (Numbers 23:19, AMPC).

And as the French say, "En Suivant La Verite," which means follow the path of truth. May we always find ourselves doing that.

"Prayer breaks all bars, dissolves all chains, opens all prisons, and widens all straits by which God's saints have been held."
—Edward Mckendree Bounds

"They who dive in the sea of affliction bring up rare pearls."
—Charles Spurgeon

Reclaiming Prayer

Precious Father, how You long for our freedom. Your heart has grieved in watching us suffer. The beauty of free will You bestow on Your children breaks Your heart when it's used for harm and not good. The wrong choices mankind has made in all its freedom have caused much sorrow and harm. Still, Your Word tells us this comforting truth: what You have spoken, You will make good.

Chapter 4

Medley of Satan's Greatest Hits

The Lord Understands You

"... Your understanding of me brings wonder and strength."
—Psalm 139:6 (TPT)

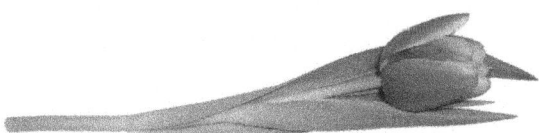

The Enemy's Greatest Hits

A medley of greatest hits sounds exciting, unless we are talking of a compilation of some of the greatest hits the enemy's dealt against us in our lifetime. Sharp blows to our emotional wellbeing, health, family, finances, or wherever his one-two punch packs the best wallop, desiring nothing more than to clean our clock. Studying our weaknesses like a trained fighter, looking for those exposed areas with the clout of an astute learner, he chomps at the bit, eager to pin us down until we tap out or cry uncle.

Let's spend some time looking at how the enemy used fear to land some-power-packed punches in my life. The good news is, God is always with us. He took all our hits, even the one-hit wonders—the ones that we wondered what hit us—turning them into His masterful remix. Carefully removing, adding, changing the original state we were left in after taking a sucker punch to the gut, He turns those punches in the gut to glory. And not only that, but God also gives us maneuverability in the ring to spiritually float like a butterfly and sting like a bee so the enemy's hands can't hit what his eyes can't see – just like Muhammad Ali.

"Surely, He has borne our griefs (sicknesses, weaknesses, and distresses) and carried our sorrows and pains [of punishment], yet we [ignorantly] considered Him stricken, smitten, and afflicted by God [as if with leprosy]. But He was wounded for our transgressions, He was bruised for our guilt and iniquities; the chastisement [needful to obtain] peace and well-being for us was upon Him, and with the stripes [that wounded] Him we are healed and made whole" (Isaiah 53:4-5, AMPC).

Somber Music

Fear took a huge toll on my life, intensely rooted in all the sexual abuses I endured growing up. The abuse was woven throughout my life, coming from family members, a professional, a classmate, a Sunday school teacher, and a boss' son. Each abuse came from people I had once trusted. A sexual predator looks for someone from a broken family going through a rough time or someone who has less of a community. They also pick people lacking confidence, making it easier to groom them (oxygen.com).

A victimizer will search for a victim. So, my first wrong touch became a catalyst that opened the door for others to walk through. They saw an opportunity. Perhaps, if that secret had been exposed early on, it might have changed the amount of abuse I endured. Only God knows, and I trust Him with turning every evil into something good.

The Scales Of Injustice

The abuse made me feel alone, worthless, and dirty; I felt so much shame. It took everything within me to hold my head above water. Any abuse is a breeding ground for fear and a host of other cohorts such as shame, distrust, and low self-esteem. Our ability to trust is on shaky ground. If sexual abuse were placed on a double-pan scale, one side could represent situations we do not label as abuse, so they remain unresolved (therefore in a state of unforgiveness), while the other side is heavily weighted down by repressed memories of traumatic events we unconsciously store in our minds, blocked from normal conscious recall, which also naturally remains unforgiven (Wikipedia). My scale had both: unresolved offenses and repressed memories, tipping the scale with a mysterious gravity.

The strange thing was, I could look at other people's lives and see the bruises abuse can produce, but still, I could not detect it in myself in survival mode. I didn't know what I was trying to survive from. I employed different coping strategies to draw comfort from to soothe the gnawing beast of pain. Whether it was food, male attention, performance, or perfectionism, I did whatever it took to silence the demons.

My body image and overall self-worth was wretched, and shame took a huge portion of my energy as I tried to hide it. We will cover more on shame in Chapter 8. However, for now, covering up shame to appear flawless is a useless endeavor, for every human being has flaws. Our attempt to pretend otherwise only robs us of relatability and the vulnerability needed to foster our healing. It also leaves us with sharp edges, as Skin Horse explained to Velveteen Rabbit in his quest to be real.

Every human has flaws. Covering up shame to appear flawless is useless.

Real Can't Be Ugly

"Real isn't how you are made," said Skin Horse. "It's a thing that happens to you. When a child loves you for a long, long time, not just to play with, but **REALLY** loves you, then you become real."

"Does it hurt?" asked the rabbit.

"Sometimes," said the Skin Horse, for he was always truthful. "When you are real, you don't mind being hurt."

"Does it happen all at once, like being wound up? Or bit by bit?" asked the rabbit.

"It doesn't happen all at once," said Skin Horse. "You become. It takes a long time. That's why it doesn't happen often to people who break easily or have sharp edges, or who have to be carefully kept. Generally, by the time you are real, most of your hair has been loved off, and your eyes drop out, and you get loose in the joints and very shabby. But these things don't matter at all because once you are real, you can't be ugly, except to people who don't understand."

I'm so grateful for all the people in my life who taught me the beauty of being real, my husband being my biggest support in it, next to Jesus.

Claimed Baggage

When my husband and I got married, the amount of baggage we carried in was substantial, and if we had our bags checked at the airport, it would have far exceeded the weight limit. However, we had each other, and most importantly, we had God. We loved and longed to serve God with all our hearts.

We had big plans to serve God in big ways, envisioning Evel Knievel-like stunts for Jesus. Instead, we got a big wheel kiddy version, hardly the grandiose results I had once hoped for. And yet when I look back, unpacking our bags (sorting through all the lies, abuse, and pain, determined to walk in wholeness), it was like jumping over the Grand Canyon, a feat in and of itself. I look back with gratefulness, knowing we did the best we could with what we had. Trying our best to draw a line in the sand to contend for our healing, we wanted the least amount of collateral damage to affect our children.

Our memories of growing up weren't all bad of course, but we prayed our children would not have to walk through any similar hardships we faced. I believe that is every loving parent's wish for their children. My mom took extra care not to do things that wounded her while growing up. Our children will most likely do things differently based on their experiences growing up. I'm all about forward movement, growth, and freedom. With God's help, we can overcome and improve with each passing generation, gaining momentum and lost ground once stolen by the enemy. All the while we can serve extra portions of grace to our imperfections. Breathe in the sacred breath of Jesus' grace.

We not only get to unpack our overcrowded, unnecessary baggage with the help of a loving God, but we also get to pack up a splendid new suitcase crammed to the brim with the good things of God, ready for any new adventure.

> *"As soon as I saw you, I knew a grand adventure was about to happen."*
> —Winnie The Pooh

For Better Or Worse

Starry-eyed, full of anticipation and excitement, repeating your vows of for better or for worse, you don't expect the worst to be on your honeymoon. Oh sure, we have heard of honeymoons going awry - getting sick, bad hotel, or storms. These situations are no fun, especially right out of the wedding-bliss starting gate. But for me and my husband, the capricious storm was internal, and that perfect storm landed right in me as I lay on the hotel bed in Newport, Oregon, Kevin's hometown.

It was like two champagne glasses raised to toast new beginnings, only to crash to the ground instead, shattering on earth's impact. The celebration turned to shards of glass and a sense of bewilderment as to what happened. That perfect storm that brewed in me started with fear. Fear was locked away in a compartment I wanted to forget, but the honeymoon seemed to have the compartment's key.

The cheating high school boyfriend I planned to marry and my cheating first husband confirmed what I already felt about myself: I am unlovable, less than, and certainly cannot captivate a man to love me with total commitment or loyalty. The interactions I had with men built the case that they could not be trusted. My sweet husband was innocent, yet he paid the price for all the other men who increased my already-distorted view of myself and my distrust of all men in general.

And on that lovely night after consummating our marriage, voices in my head were telling me to jump out the window. Being a visual person, I could imagine my body sprawled on the cold pavement, the sounds of the waves crashing in the distance, while the sea breeze brushed across my lifeless body...the soft glow from a lamp post shone down on me.

Dramatic, yes, yet so was my reality. Immediately, I shared with Kevin the horrific thoughts tormenting my mind, which is not what one would want to hear, ever, especially on their honeymoon.

I cannot praise God enough for a loving, supportive, and faithful husband who has stood by me through it all. His tenacious love for God brought me through my darkest hours. I want to encourage you that "God shows no partiality, undue favor or unfairness; with Him one man is not different from another" (Romans 2:11, AMPC).

So, though I received healing from God through Kevin, we do not need a husband or wife to obtain our healing, unless that is part of God's plan. God will use different means to bring us healing in His time and ways. He is ready to answer the cry and desire of our heart, for it is His heart's desire to free us completely. Keep seeking, asking, and knocking, and you will find your deliverance.

False Evidence

Satan works hand in hand with false evidence and accusations, for he is known to be the accuser of brethren day and night. His bag of tricks is tried and tested. Sad to say, I fell for them more than a time or two.

The thought of being cheated on again reared its ugly head so high and fierce that I yielded to its magnetic force. That false evidence became real to me, and I doubted Kevin's loyalty time after time, though he pled his innocence. He did not commit a crime, but I had tried him as guilty. I was comparing apples to oranges, throwing them in the same bag, weighing them on the cheating scale. Many times, I asked for a divorce to save face. Being rejected again was more than I could bear, so I thought I would be proactive. Mind you, this was all false evidence that appeared very real to me. I believed a lie, hook, line, and sinker, and it was sinking me.

One night, early in our marriage, Kevin was running a little late from work, and I was convinced he was cheating on me. Grabbing my purse, I jumped in my car and headed to my parents' house down the road. As I was pulling out, Kevin was pulling in, and he looked shocked; it was 11:00 at night. He was looking forward to coming home and snuggling with his wife after a long, hard day of work, but I was getting out of Dodge based on some lie that spun out of control. With intense fear and red-hot anger coursing through my body, I accused him of infidelity, then rolled up the window and drove away to the sounds of his pleas and denials. My heart did not want to go, but my head so full of lies said something completely different. Fear was in the driver's seat, and I was going along for the ride.

As I pulled out of the long parking lot of our apartment building, I looked in the rear-view mirror to see my beloved husband running after me. That picture broke me. What a picture of love, for God chases us down to prove His love when we are unable to trust, are full of skepticism, and feel completely broken. I stopped, pulled around and came back home to a man who had my heart and—slowly, through a long season—eventually my trust.

My husband proved himself faithful countless times, even though I put him through the wringer. How I longed to understand this foreign language of unconditional love that had no strings attached or rejection as its final destination. He was patient, even when I knew I had to be trying his patience. Innumerable times his relentless love from God to me kept pursuing me, even when I was subconsciously sabotaging our marriage, acting on lies I was convinced were true.

My identity was ironclad in fiction, based solely on a handful of men who did not have the capacity to love me. The truth was, they could simply not duly love, not because I was unlovable. I, too, have hurt people in a relationship out of brokenness or realizing they were not the right ones for me. The same holds true for those who have hurt me. I can only hope for grace and forgiveness to those I have hurt.

Another Hook

Kevin and I had been married for almost five years, and turbulent waters of jealously and fear of him leaving me subsided greatly to where I was ready to have a baby. On March 14th, 1992, we were blessed with our beautiful son Derek. Our joy knew no bounds, for he was purely delightful.

And then, just a short 28 months later, we welcomed our precious son Trent into the world. Looking at his sweet little face, my life and family felt complete. Those two are such a gift; they are one of the best things that have happened to me.

Fear was always a part of my life in one form or another, and it did not take long to realize fear was going to cling on for dear life, trying to take me and my family down.

It reminds me of when I was young; my family and cousins went to Champoeg State Park one day on a whim. I did not have the tennis shoes I usually wore in the river because of the sharp rocks, but I was game to jump in with my cousin Dori. We splashed, swam, and giggled, moving about freely in the river's refreshing waters as the warm sunshine gave a nod of approval.

Suddenly, something was tugging at my foot. Pulling it up from the glistening waters to examine it, I saw a rusty fishhook stuck in my big toe, with the fishing line still attached to it, held under a rock. I did not have the nerve to get it out on my own. I yelled out to my dad, who was on the shore, to come help me. He came to my rescue and removed the rusty hook from my toe and the fishing line from the rock it was stuck under, freeing me from its limitations. The hook of fear was something I was not able to get rid of on my own.

Satan's Victory Laps

It did not take long to see that the normal fears other moms had did not match up to mine. Mine were bigger, worse, and far more beastly. Now, I needed to guard my children with my life. They could not be watched by anyone but my mom, neither could they go anywhere without me...that included with my husband, yes, their own flesh-and-blood father. My heart hurts to think of it even today. As if having to prove his innocence was not enough in regard to him cheating, he had to live with the fact that he could not take his boys anywhere without me, for still in my brokenness, I feared men could not be fully trusted.

Scanning the horizon for any mother like me, I found none. It became very apparent that I was not normal, neither was this way of thinking normal. The tears I cried to be free were plenty; the pain I saw I was causing felt insurmountable. Racking my brain as to why I could not let Kevin take the boys anywhere, the only lame reason that came to mind was, "What if they got in a car accident, and they needed me?" That is not even logical, for I could die in the accident too. However, the fear and lack of understanding was the best I had. It was like pulling your pockets inside out for coins, only to find lint.

As the years went by, the need to control was greater, and the push back understandably elevated. When Kevin would ask to take the children, I could not do it. The fear was so overpowering that I resorted to thinking I needed a divorce. In my twisted thinking, that would force me to let him be with the children alone.

The prayers going up to God for freedom were far too numerous. Thankfully, my prayer postures were not always on my knees, thus avoiding the nickname "Old Camel Knees," which was the title given to the author of the book of James. The hours in prayer on his knees toughened them up like a camel's as he interceded. Whew! I dodged a bullet on that one. Though, honestly, I would have taken those crusty knees in a heartbeat in exchange for my freedom.

The amount of hate I had in my heart for what I was doing felt as crusty and hard as James' knees, with a toughness that seemed impenetrable, for I simply saw no relief in sight.

Eventually, when the boys reached a certain age, they could go with their dad without me, though they still grew up home-schooled and overly protected. It was not until years later, looking back, when I became aware that those stupid lint balls of lies were actually a vow I made: I would never let my children suffer being sexually abused. That vow was an undetected inroad I had carved out of self-preservation. It was paved in fear and did not come to life until it was excavated from the depths of my buried pain.

Love Of God And Family

I'm not just thankful to God and Kevin for their tender care; I also thank God for my boys who have forgiven me, while also encouraging me to overcome my fears like going on the big, scary rides at amusement parks. Both are needed to spur me on to greater healing.

I have thanked Derek many times for his push to ride a rollercoaster, which helped me overcome my fear to take a risk. Because of his gentle, loving nudge, I enjoyed something I never would have otherwise. And I did apologize for saying he was grounded as I careened down the Ghostrider Wooden Roller Coaster...I was only joking, mostly...

And Trent's encouraging words have helped me slow down when I was in my vroom vroom mode. His support has moved me into the slower lane countless times. My sons have and forever will be such a blessing to me.

My heart is full of love for my family. They have walked an extremely difficult path and found it in their hearts to forgive, extend grace, and still love me. Miraculously, they saw through all my brokenness, seeing my sincere heart of love for them. I know it was no easy task. I'm completely undone with God's profound love and that of my family's. It brings me to tears every time I think of it.

Henry Cloud said, "We can't undo the hurt someone has caused us, but we can let go of it." I'm beyond grateful they did that for me. My manly men could sing "Let It Go" (from Disney's *Frozen* movie) in three-part harmony.

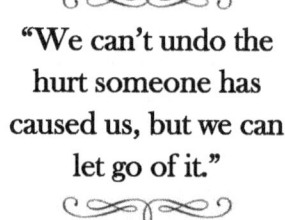

"We can't undo the hurt someone has caused us, but we can let go of it."

Let Fear Go

"There is no room in love for fear. Well-formed love banishes fear. Since fear is crippling, a fearful life—fear of death, fear of judgment—is one not yet fully formed in love" (1 John 4:18, MSG).

Terrarium Of Fear

Living in a terrarium of fear, your world is tiny, constrictive, and musty. You look out your glass house through occasionally foggy windows mingled with stagnant air. All the while, the top lid is screwed on, tight as a drum. You're unable to get free from your stuffy accommodations unless someone pulls you out to freedom and fresh air.

A funny thing happened while I was looking up how to spell *terrarium* correctly. I accidentally said *terrarium of fear* into my phone as my search. It just so happens, at this very moment, Esty is selling a beautiful locket with a faux stone heart inside that reads "Give in to love or live in fear." How cool is that! I want one; God never ceases to amaze me.

I have made terrariums before with our Sunday school class and by myself in our car. How does one build a terrarium in their car? It is quite simple. It all started when I chopped down a holly tree located at the west side of our house, one branch at a time. Loping each branch laden with holly berries, I then crammed them into 30-gallon paper lawn bags. After these 30-gallon bags were full, I loaded them into our black Buick, which years later our son Trent told me he thought was a limousine. It certainly could look like one to a three-year-old.

Before you clutch your pearls, let me explain a tad further. We had no truck at that time and saw no other way to get all those branches to the yard recycling center. Actually, you know what? Go ahead and clutch those pearls. What were we thinking? In fact, if I were wearing pearls, I would clutch them too.

Our highly unconventional and now seemingly quite foolish way of disposing of yard debris was on a downhill slope from conception. That bad idea became a flat-out fiasco, for after we finished loading up, our limousine would not start! Unbelievable! Dead in the water with enough holly branches to supply a nursery through the holiday season. Our car had to sit for a couple of days; our windows fogged up and dampness in the air made the car smell of mildewy holly branches and moss. Not my go-to for an air freshener.

Looking back on this silly story, I'm wondering why we did not unload the car at that time. Perhaps our reason was no garage and paper bags in the rain? Who knows. But then, what can you expect? You're reading a story of someone cramming 30-gallon bags of holly into a Buick. Enough said! Just thinking of this story actually makes me laugh out loud; the whole thing is so ludicrous.

The point is, our old Buick, aka the limousine, was not meant to carry yard debris; it was not designed for this. Its creator had plans of smooth rides, comfortable seats, and getting the consumer to their destination with style. So, too, your loving Heavenly Father did not create us to carry sin debris or live in a terrarium of fear as our ecosystem. Instead, He wants us to "give in to love and not live in fear." My wrong google search gave the right answer, after all.

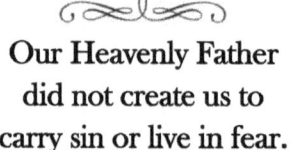
Our Heavenly Father did not create us to carry sin or live in fear.

Fear clouds our vision and cramps our style, keeping us from getting to our destination, just as it is wrong on so many levels to stuff holly branches in a luxury limousine. I can see clearly now; now that the windows are no longer fogged up.

Hitting The Panic Button

Peering through the sweating glass house of fear—living, breathing, marinating in it—is not helpful, neither is it healthy for our wellbeing. My body began to suffer from all the fear, trying to control a world that is on most accounts uncontrollable. Finally, I made a visit to a naturopathic doctor, and a new diet to follow was set in place. My out-of-control eating habits needed a makeover. The four main food groups of Buddy the Elf—candy, candy canes, candy corn, and syrup—sounded just all right with me, plus the occasional pasta carbs for good measure. My body, however, had understandable objections.

That simple change of eating less sugar tripped my body into full-blown panic attacks. One day, out of the blue, my mind became foggy and my surroundings surreal, borderline dream-like. It felt as if I was a balloon floating aimlessly through life; nothing seemed grounded. To be left alone put such fear in my heart it seemed unbearable. My panic was at code-red level when I was unable to get ahold of Dr. Collins over the weekend. I was certain I had lost my mind.

My dad had a nervous breakout when I was 15. It had always been my fear that one day, my mind could snap like a twig just as his did. My heart was also breaking to look at our sweet boys, who were five and three at the time, wondering if my brain would ever feel normal again.

Crying out to God, I begged for my healing and answers. That weekend, at the grocery store, I picked up a women's magazine to try to get my mind off my mind. Lo and behold, there was an article about one woman's journey with panic attacks, and guess what? They can be brought on by a change in diet. By the time I got to talk to Dr. Collins, I had already realized what had happened to me, and he confirmed my God-given diagnosis.

Also, that same weekend, God had another divine appointment. My mom sat by a lovely woman at church, who just so happened to have suffered from panic attacks. She graciously loaned me her whole cassette tape series discussing tools to overcome anxiety. I still remember, huddled in our converted garage, while the boys played, I worked through getting well. It was not overnight that my foggy brain went away, but I knew it would be okay with the Lord's help, and that's all I needed to know.

The Perfect Landing

Though I have countless stories of my crippling walk with fear, today I can write that God has brought me deep, abiding peace and freedom. Do I still struggle with fear at times? Yes, I do. I'm human, and I'm still learning to take thoughts captive to the obedience of Jesus Christ. I'm actively digging into my toolbox to get the proper tools when something triggers me. At times, I feel like Simone Bile, with my mental gymnastics of what is truth and what is a lie, thrilled when I land a double-double dismount on the balance beam of life.

What's important is to put one foot in front of the other every day, hands chalked to grip God's Word. A firm grip helps reduce the friction of everyday life. God is completely trustworthy, faithful, and kind. His score card for your performance is a perfect ten. He knows your heart and is well-pleased coaching you to gold-medal victory.

Overcoming Fear: Spiritual Training Verses

"... keep your thoughts continually fixed on all that is authentic and real, honorable and admirable, beautiful and respectful, pure and holy, merciful and kind. And fasten your thoughts on every glorious work of God, praising him always. Follow the example of all that we have imparted to you and the God of peace will be with you in all things" (Philippians 4:8, TPT).

"Joyful is the person who finds wisdom, the one who gains understanding. For wisdom is more profitable than silver, and her wages are better than gold. Wisdom is more precious than rubies, nothing you desire can compare with her. She offers you long life in her right hand, and riches and honor in her left, She will guide you down delightful paths; all her ways are satisfying. Wisdom is a tree of life to those who embrace her; happy are those who hold her tightly" (Proverbs 3:13, NLT).

"And God-Enthroned spoke to me and said, 'Consider this! I am making everything to be new and fresh. Write down at once all that I have told you, because each word is trustworthy and dependable'" (Rev 21:5, TPT).

Re-VERSE Your Captivity

"Behold, at that time I will deal with all those who afflict you; I will save the limping [ones] and gather the outcasts and will make them a praise and a name in every land of their shame. At that time I will bring you in; yes, at that time I will gather you, for I will make you a name and a praise among all the nations of the earth when I reverse your captivity before your eyes, says the Lord" (Zephaniah 3:19-20, AMPC).

That somber melody fades away and is replaced with sweet singing, a joyful noise unto the Lord, just like His Word promises.

From our *Whys* to God of Wonders

1. Make a list of your fears, starting with your biggest. Then tell each one to go in the name and blood of Jesus.

_____

_____

_____

2. Wield your sword: Memorize scripture verses to combat your fears and speak them out in agreement.

"For we have the living Word of God, which is full of energy, and it pierces more sharply than a two-edged sword. It will even penetrate to the very core of our being where soul and spirit, bone and marrow meet It interprets and reveals the true thoughts and secret motives of our hearts" (Hebrews 4:12, TPT).

3. Have others pray for you: When you come up to battle your fears, have Godly warriors come alongside and lift you in prayer... for tremendous power is released through the passionate, heartfelt prayer of a godly believer!" (James 5:16, TPT).

4. Baby steps: Take a baby step whenever you can to overcome your fears. They do lessen when you see they are not as big as you thought they were.

5. Reward yourself: Do something that speaks to your spirit to celebrate your steps toward freedom. I started a charm bracelet of hope and healing, buying charms to either make a declaration of what God was doing or already had done. One was a silver rubber ducky with a tiny baby shoe. Everything was just ducky, even in my baby steps. God was cheering me on with each wobbly step, rejoicing in my progress. He is doing the same with you, my friend.

6. Declare and decree His love for you: Speak how much He loves you, how delighted He is in you. Write down on a 3x5 card positive truths of His love for you. Then, speak them out loud in agreement.

"Everything you want is on the other side of fear." —Jack Canfield

"I learned that courage was not absence of fear but the triumph over it. The brave man is not he who does not feel afraid, but he who conquers that fear." —Nelson Mandela

Reclaiming Prayer

Precious Father, we thank You that Your perfect love casts out fear and all the torment that comes with it. Help us to receive Your love like a prized gift, elated to not only open it but display it, use it, and wear it. For Your love is the best gift ever, and not only does it dispel fear, but it also comes with an eternal lifetime guarantee.

Chapter 5

The Not-So-Funhouse Mirror

The Lord Shaped You

"You even formed every bone in my body when you created me in the secret place carefully, skillfully shaping me from nothing to something."
—Psalm 139:15 (TPT)

Mirror, Mirror

When my brother Troy was alive, he was a big kid at heart. He loved God and his family with a boyish grin and an infectious laugh. Sadly, his Lewy Body dementia began to affect his movement, speech, thinking, and behavior.

As the disease progressed, his speech became more difficult to understand. Anytime I could decipher what he was trying to communicate, his eyes lit up, and a smile graced his face. Whenever I could not, my only solution was to offer him a nod and smile, hoping it was the right response to whatever he was trying to share with me at the time. It was heartbreaking to watch his once strong body with its normal abilities being carried away in the torrent of this ruthless disease.

No longer able to return my hugs, his arms were unable to reciprocate the gesture. Yet, even though all the vibrant and basic parts of his life were slipping away, my brother remained the kind and even joyful soul he had always been and did so courageously until his death.

He had been affectionately called Geppetto for his love for vintage toys, marionette puppets, and all the clever things he did when he taught children for Sunday school. He loved playing his guitar, tinkering with vintage cars, and thrift store shopping for quirky items. For a season, he made fun house mirrors, creating them with brightly colored wooden frames. You know the ones that make you look like you have legs to the sky or hips that could reach across a continent? Yep, those gems can make you laugh until your sides split. However, it is no laughing matter when we have a distorted image of ourselves because of the lies the enemy whispers in our ears in regard to our body image. Our thoughts can become as warped as a manipulated mirror.

Don't Quote Me On This

I have no doubt when Wallis Simpson, the Duchess of Windsor, uttered her famous quote, "You can never be too rich or too thin." She had no idea how sorely misguided she was in regard to the subject of weight.

Do not think I'm throwing a stone at her in judgment; I'm not. I laid my stones down when I realized I thought like she did, and at one time, I lived it. For me, being super thin was in, and the less you weighed, the more self-worth you attained. This was a silly game I played in hopes of winning approval. Unfortunately, the game of self-worth Monopoly always landed me in jail, a prison of lies with no get-out-of-jail-free cards in sight.

Too Thin Was In

As I wrote earlier, I had issues with my body image most of my life. In fact, I had issues with myself in general. How I longed to be like Twiggy, the swinging teenage model in the sixties. She was tall and skinny, and I felt short and not so thin. My precious childhood friend Janet was like that: tall, stately, long, slender legs that never appeared to spread out like a generous helping of jam on toast when she sat down (as I felt mine did).

The funny thing was, when I told her as an adult how I longed for her figure, she told me I had a thing or two she admired. We can struggle so much in our lack of self-worth we don't see the beauty God has given us.

When we struggle with self-worth, we don't see the beauty God has given us.

My self-esteem was so low I saw little value in myself. How God longs for us to celebrate being made in His image. The wrap-around presence of the altogether lovely One is a wonderful place to see your priceless worth and value.

Comfort In Food

As I grew older, food became more of a comfort that filled a place in my soul where a gnawing spiritual starvation resided. Try as I may, it could never be fully satisfied with heaping piles of mashed potatoes or a Snickers candy bar.

In my mind, I was fat and unlovable; those feelings only intensified as a hormonal teenager. Whenever I stood at the bottom landing of our split-level home to say goodbye to my mom, like clockwork, I would turn to leave, uttering, "I know you think I'm fat." She never once said anything to me about my weight. My warped body image, like a not-so-fun-house mirror, was quite convincing, causing me to believe everyone saw me like I saw myself.

My poor mama would say, "Lisa, I'm just saying goodbye to you." Then, in her anguish, she would blurt out, "Pick a fat friend!" Closing the door, my heart grieved with what I was putting my mom through. All my self-loathing simply refused to go away, for I chose to say goodbye to truth and reality and begrudgingly welcome a lie instead. I was feeling so mad at myself for my behavior, while shaking my head at my mother's desperate attempt to remedy it.

And for those wondering, no, I did not hunt for a friend who liked to eat as much as I did. Although...I did sign up for Camp Fire Girls at age ten because my friend said they were serving brownies. True Story! It just so happens, I recently found out what the Camp Fire slogan was for its 50th anniversary. It was: "She Cares...Do you?" Apparently, if it involved brownies, I most certainly did!

Mister Wrong

When I began to date, a good number of guys I went out with had an opinion of how I should look, what I should wear, how I needed to lose weight, tone my leg muscles, etc. The list of areas I could improve was long, hurtful, and too exhausting to attain. Bobbing up and down in my own sea of unworthiness, I was allowing others' points of view toward me to pound against the S.S. Shameful that I was already hopelessly trying to stand upright on. This life's excursion rivaled Gilligan's Island S.S. Minnow's, where a hope for a three-hour sightseeing tour went horribly wrong.

Looking for love and acceptance in others' opinions will land you shipwrecked on a desert island of emotional insecurities, unstable as sinking sand. Until we find our true north—our inherent worth in Jesus Christ—we cannot live in our true, God-given identity. He is an anchor for our tossed soul, securing our self-worth in Christ alone, far removed from every whim of public opinion. Our need for approval is met in Christ alone. And the Lord said to me one day, "If we play to an audience of one, we will always have a sold-out crowd." He is sold out to you.

"If we play to an audience of one, we will always have a sold-out crowd."

"We have this certain hope like a strong, unbreakable anchor holding our souls to God himself. Our anchor of hope is fastened to the mercy seat which sits in the heavenly realm beyond the sacred threshold" (Hebrews 6:19, TPT).

Starving For Attention

My body image and low self-esteem rumbled like an overactive volcano.

Have you heard about Mount St. Helens? In 1980, that dormant volcano finally blew, spewing 500 million tons of ash with its eruption. Some of its ash was found as far as 2,000 miles away on the plains in Oklahoma.

My eruption happened when my high school sweetheart took a liking to an exotic, dark-skinned, dark-haired beauty who worked next door to Merle Normans cosmetics, where I worked. His decision to break up with me became my Mount St. Helens moment. Ironically, I watched that eruption from my 1975 Mustang in the parking lot of that same mall months later on May 18th, 1980.

Looking back, I should have seen the signs that I was not his cup of tea. One evening, I remember that striking beauty sashaying over from the Foxmoor clothing store where she worked to borrow our store's vacuum cleaner. My boyfriend was hanging out in the backroom, talking to me as I rolled the vacuum out to miss cutie patootie, only to find out from him afterward that I had a sticker stuck on my booty. Yep, that is how I roll, with serious vacuum-cleaner swag. Of course, it was no ordinary blasé sticker. If you're going to make a fool of yourself with a sticker on your butt, do so with a bold declaration like "Keep away from heat flammable." Make sure it's perfectly centered on your bum like a bullseye. I say, "Go big or go home."

Let me just tell you, this apple did not fall far from the tree. I have to tell you a couple stories. My sweet mama once had a "$2.50 a pair" sticker on her breasts from leaning against the pillowcases I was trying to sell at a Flea Market. I gently had to say, "Mom, I don't think you want to sell those for that," pointing to her chest. Fortunately, my mom was wonderful at laughing at herself, which came in handy a time or two. Shortly after that mishap, she shined brightly again when our family got the check for the delicious meal we finished at Sayler's Old Country Kitchen. As mom looked at the bill, she blurted out loudly, "My breasts were 7.95!" My dad looked at her in shock. Indeed, it would have been much less unexpected if she had added the word "chicken" to her sentence. I, however, found the perfect opportunity to add, "Wow! Mom, they really went up in price." You go, girl!

There were times as a teenager I longed to be classy and dignified, not wanting to draw attention to myself with embarrassing gaffs. Until one day, it became blatantly obvious I was fighting a losing battle. I chose to embrace it instead, for anything else is pure futility. I began learning to laugh at myself and all my faux pas; celebrating them stops me from swimming against the current of how God created me.

In fact, now I cannot wait to tell my friend Debbie whenever I do something goofy. She laughs at the comical predicaments I find myself in. She is the Ethel to my Lucy moments. What once brought shame, now brings uninhibited joy excavated from its ruins. And Mom, about that waving hand that you stuck on your forehead, giving you a hickey, I think it is completely hilarious now! If only I could tell you so...

It Sucks To Be Cheated On

So, about that boy, Kevin, who dumped me for the girl next door, it made my small world fall apart. Somehow, food made me think of our times together, and I could barely eat. My weight dropped just as my spirits had.

In our two-year relationship, we had plans to get married after we graduated. In fact, the day after he had told my mom he wanted to marry me, he was buying me a sweater (wink wink) from the beauty who borrowed my vacuum cleaner. Eventually, I'm sure my boyfriend was using the clever line, "Can I borrow your vacuum cleaner?" A likely story.

Though my boyfriend and I made numerous attempts to mend our relationship, it eventually failed, for he had a hard time remaining faithful. Those pretty girls behind the wheels of those Dysons, Hoovers, and Bissells were just too tempting to resist. Feeling like I was one vacuum cleaner away from being dumped was kind of a deal-breaker, because it sucks like a Dyson VII Torque Drive to be cheated on.

Mister Right

Looking back, I tell people I just had the wrong Kevin. God has a sense of humor, for *Mr. Right* Kevin not only had the same name, but he also had the same birthday and year as *Mr. Wrong* Kevin. Not that I was looking for that, of course.

And to put a cherry on top, the jobs I had after high school eventually led me back to becoming the manager of the very same clothing store at Mall 205 where cheating heart *Mr. Wrong* wooed the exotic beauty.

And drum roll, please...that very same store where my heart was broken became the very same store my heart would begin to heal. Full-circle redemption, for my new friend Kevin, who I had met at a church college career group three years prior, found me there one day after we'd lost contact for over a year. My eyes instantly opened to see him in a whole new light. He was out of the friend zone in a New York minute as he made his way into the store that day.

Shortly after, the Lord reminded me of a conversation I'd had over a year ago with my store's district manager, Jeff. He was a wonderful man of God, full of wisdom and counsel. One day, he visited the store while I was unpacking clothes in the stock room. Concerned, he kindly said, "Lisa, you never know, you might marry someone you already know." Perhaps I should not have laughed at that idea. God loves to bring our healing full circle. He uses the ashes at your feet to bring beauty, teeming with life, just like Mount St. Helens' rebirth of its flora and fauna. It is a wonderful sight to behold.

"For the vision is yet for an appointed time and it hastens to the end [fulfillment]; it will not deceive or disappoint. Though it tarry, wait [earnestly] for it, because it will surely come; it will not be behindhand on its appointed day" (Habakkuk 2:3, AMPC).

Though the vision tarries, wait for it.

One final wink from God that is too good not to share! The church group where I met Kevin for the first time, when I was freshly divorced (which I will explain next), broken, and struggling with an eating disorder, was called *Hineni*. It is a Hebrew word that means "Here I am." *Hineni* is a parent's response to the call of their child as seen in Genesis 22:7, 27:18, and it is a child's response to the call of their parents, as seen in Genesis 27:1, 37:13

(jewishchronicle.org). I'm so thankful God our Father responded to my cry for help, and I responded to His call with, "Here I am."

One More Heartbreak For The Road

I gave you a peek at my happy ending. Before I took a dive back into another hardship, I thought we could use a break. Being me was exhausting. Once I knew the door was slammed shut on my high school boyfriend's relationship, I ended up meeting and marrying a man who was not able to be honest or faithful just like my last boyfriend. Lather, rinse, repeat!

Married at 20, just to find myself divorced at 21, my life spun out of control with a crushing belief (now embedded deep into my soul), convinced I was not worthy of love. Somehow, what I had to offer was subpar; other women were better than me and worthy of love when I must not be. That out-of-control feeling brought me to an unreasonable conclusion. One thing I can control is what I eat. So, I began the first steps down a dark path that led me right into the arms of anorexia.

With each pound that came off, empowerment came in. To be called skinny, even anorexic, was music to my ears. My clothes now draped my skin with ease. Now, whenever I said goodbye to my mom, I felt truly thin. Sweet victory without the calories. One day, she cried as she watched me waste away, begging me to start eating, telling me my face had become so thin my teeth were showing more. My face, usually on the rounder side, was never spoken as thin. So, in my warped thinking, I hit the jackpot, and turned my face to conceal the glee. Oblivious, my celebration was leading straight to emaciation.

I was going nowhere fast, just like that bike.

In my mind, I just got the golden ticket. From feasting on M&M's and a Slurpee for dinner to eating just a can of carrots or an occasional salad, my poor body was begging for nutrition. Anytime I did eat, I rode my mom's squeaky exercise bike like a banshee. The crazy thing is, that bike had no resistance, so I was basically pedaling air. So, I was going nowhere fast, a perfect metaphor for my life at that time.

I'm profoundly grateful for a praying mom and a God who is in the business of healing us mind, body, soul, and spirit – the total package of goodness. Talk about truly a golden ticket that led to freedom. Through the faithful prayers of a loving mom, one day, my eyes were completely opened. I saw myself in very baggy pants, a sweater that engulfed my smaller frame and skinny arms that could not possibly belong to me. Gazing in that mirror scared me to wholeness. Not to mention losing lots of my hair and my menstrual cycle stopping for over a year.

This was no longer a laughing matter; it became a catalyst to convince me this was not a winning scenario. Slowly, I started giving myself permission to no longer deny or restrict vital nutrients my body needed to survive and thrive. Even though watching the weight come back on was difficult, I knew it was the right thing to do. My body could not have agreed more.

Play It Again

The enemy knows our weaknesses and will check the doors to see if they are locked, barring him from coming as an uninvited guest. As I mentioned before, my body image had been a huge battle. So, when Kevin and I got married, the birth control pills made me not only gain weight, but also it brought depression and occasional thoughts of suicide. My doctor said that was the lowest dose available, so instead of finding another form of birth control, I continued taking them for nearly five years. One day, it was no longer an option. I had a fleeting thought of ramming my Nissan into a semi-truck while taking the I-84 freeway. This was a rude awaking and the last Dixie straw that broke the camel's back.

Once I got off those pills, it became clear how much they had been affecting me emotionally. The bigger picture showed its effects not only on my marriage to Kevin but also with my first husband, making that difficult marriage even more so. I always thought my behavior was due to being overly sensitive or not strong enough. In reality, this chemical I was ingesting was causing my estrogen levels to go higher than they already were. The side effects of weight gain compounded the low self-esteem and depression, becoming a vicious bicycle built for two. Believe me; I did not look sweet upon that mode of transportation. Pants snug, along with my discouragement, made me somehow think I could take control of this out-of-control situation.

Flushing It All Away

Sometimes starting a sentence with "I can take control of this situation" does not always end well...I'm just saying. One day, I decided to take the helm of the boat after christening my ship named "I Got This," which should have been called the Titanic. I charted my own path, leaving Jesus at the shore in the wake of my poor decision.

I thought to myself, *Since I cannot seem to stop overeating, I can make myself throw up.* From the end of my rope it seemed like a good idea, though I absolutely loathed doing it. "Desperate times call for desperate measures," I said in my broken state as I made my way to the bathroom. Locking the door securely, I pulled my hair back, leaning into the toilet, wanting to rid myself of whatever was eating me up inside, flushing away my overindulgence right along with it.

The guilt was unconquerable as was the shame, and just when I began to put my fingers in my mouth to start a whole new demon called bulimia, my husband opened the door. He said, "What are you doing?" The look on his face said it all. His concern and love, coupled with the fact that he opened a well-locked door without a jiggle, was purely God's intervention. Once again, God saved me from myself and the path of destruction I seemed to be drawn to like a moth to a flame. That one wake-up call was enough for me to never attempt to do it again, ever.

Surely, Your Temple Is Beautiful

We are the temple of the Holy Spirit, and it is important to take care of ourselves. There is nothing wrong with wanting to improve certain areas. It is good to remind ourselves to do it in love and not internal angst or disapproval. Nurturing our bodies is loving ourselves and God for His amazing creation. If you're naturally skinny, yay! Enjoy it. If you're naturally curvier, yippee! Celebrate it. Even if we never struggle with our body shape, perhaps it's our hair, the shape of our nose, or the sound of our voice that brings a sense of displeasure about ourselves. God would not want us to hang out in a self-image basement. He wants us to live in His truth that says we are beautiful inside and out, glorious, one of a kind! When we are kind to ourselves, it spills out onto others. So does the overflow from taking care of ourselves. It spills to those around us, giving us the ability to love others with honor and dignity because we love ourselves with the same grace. It helps me to ask myself this question: "Would I be a friend to someone who talked as mean to me as I do to myself at times?" I don't think so.

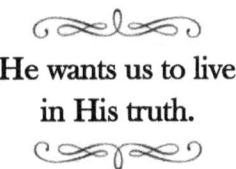

He wants us to live in His truth.

> *"May your inner voice be the kindest voice you know"*
> (next to Jesus, of course). —Author Unknown

"In that way, whatever happens to one member happens to all. If one suffers, everyone suffers. If one is honored, everyone rejoices" (1 Corinthians 12:26, TPT).

"The one I love calls to me: Arise, my dearest. Hurry, my darling. Come away with me! I have come as you have asked to draw you to my heart and lead you out. For now is the time, my beautiful one. The season has changed, the bondage of your barren winter has ended, and the season of hiding is over and gone. The rains have soaked the earth and left it bright with blossoming flowers . . . Can you not discern this new day of destiny breaking forth around you? The early signs of my purposes and plans are bursting forth. The budding vines of new life are now blooming everywhere. The fragrance of their flowers whispers, 'There is change in the air.' Arise, my love, my beautiful companion, and run with me to the higher place. For now is the time to arise and come away with me" (Song of Solomon 2:10-13 TPT).

"Listen, my dearest darling, you are so beautiful—you are beauty itself to me!" (Song of Songs 4:1, TPT).

From Our *Whys* To God's Wonders

Loving The Skin You're In

Do you have any warped images or thoughts about yourself? Take some time to write them down.

_____
_____
_____

Now, write about how God sees you.

_____
_____
_____

Find a mirror reflection verse that shows the Father's heart toward you, gazing on that truth as your new God-given image.

_____
_____
_____

Remember, no longer listen to the lies that resort to your image distort.

"Every piece of you is a burst of beautiful." —Author Unknown

"There is nothing more rare, nor more beautiful, than a woman being apologetically herself; comfortable in her perfect imperfection. To me, that is the true essence of beauty." —Steve Maraboli

"Sparkle, Shirley." —Gertrude Temple

There are many famous people who talk about embracing your jiggly or wobbly bits, and I think that is sound advice. Love all of your seeming imperfections.

Reclaiming Prayer

Father God, how You delight in us! You created each one of us with Your DNA, Your fingerprint of love. As sons and daughters of the Most High God, we have designer genes that reflect the glory of You to everyone we meet. Help us to see beauty in ourselves and others, celebrating and embracing the wabi-sabi in all of us.

Chapter 6

You Do You, Boo

The Lord Knows Your Inner Being

"You read my heart like an open book and you know all the words I'm about to speak before I even start a sentence! You know every step I will take before my journey even begins."
—Psalm 139:4 (TPT)

The God Of Green Hope

Whenever comparison shows up on the scene, it most likely has a couple of sick kicks called envy and jealousy. These three musketeers shout, "All for one, and one for all!" as they charge into our lives, burying joy under the destructive rumble of their noxious attention-grabbing for significance.

As you may already know, envy means longing for what someone else has, thus making you green with envy. The little green-eyed monster known as jealousy stems from feeling threatened, thinking what we have will be taken away. At times in my life, I went from being a Christ-loving, Jesus-following person into the Incredible Hulk. An unwelcoming bruteness formed from comparison, morphing me into a vivid shade of green, either by envy or jealousy. This always caught me by surprise; it's a place I simply never wanted my heart to go.

If we don't know our value in Christ Jesus, we can allow those feelings to get drummed up; if we lose sight of our worth in Christ (who alone is more than enough) and our insecurities go unchecked, they become a petri dish cultivating comparison in our lives. Choosing to walk in the truth of God's love for us, coupled with daily gratitude, can prevent envy or jealousy from entering our spiritual culture plate. Walking in our God-given identity, we will no longer view the grass as being greener on the other side. The color of someone else's grass is a mere illusion from the enemy to derail us.

Let's recognize these falsehoods he tries to trip us up with. Instead, let's remain in the lush meadows the Good Shepherd provides for us recorded in Psalm 23:2-3 (MSG). "God, my shepherd! I don't need a thing You have bedded me down in lush meadows, you find me quiet pools to drink from. True to your word, you let me catch my breath and send me in the right direction." This verse reminds us to be content as we tend to our own grass, keeping it green, and watering it with gratitude and truth.

"Oh! May the God of green hope fill you up with joy, fill you up with peace, so that your believing lives, filled with the life-giving energy of the Holy Spirit, will brim over with hope!" (Romans 15:13, MSG).

Some redemption for very bad rap of the color green. This is a green we can get behind.

Poisonous Apple

Once we bite into the lie of comparison, just like Eve, our eyes are open to a whole new way of thinking. For Eve, one minute she stood in the most beautiful garden with total access to the Lord's presence, completely naked and unafraid. The next minute, she was hiding to cover her shame of nakedness, feeling exposed. Comparison makes us want to run for cover, shrink back, feel inadequate and unqualified. Our God-given identity plummets as our eyes turn toward our lack rather than to God's abundance toward us.

Comparison makes us feel inadequate and unqualified.

It can be easy to get tricked by the enemy, just like Eve, if we are not careful. Genesis 3:1 (AMPC) describes the serpent as more crafty (subtle and skilled in deceit). Eve formed her lips around the forbidden fruit, coaxed by the serpent's subtlety. Comparing ourselves with others erodes our calling and purpose, and it can start with one bite of a lie. Thankfully, when we choose to ground ourselves in the truth of God's love, we chuck the bad apple along with the lie that wormed its way into our thinking. Then, we emerge from our false identity and insecurities to experience being fully loved by God, completely aware of our worth, value, purpose. His paths open wide, and we get to move forward, unobstructed, toward our God-given destiny once and for all. We are no longer concerned about the enemy handing us shiny apples like the evil queen telling Snow White, "Go on, have a bite." We have tasted the goodness of God and can boldly say, "Devil, no, not today."

The Road Map

For all my life, I struggled with comparison. It's like building a false sense of acceptance on unstable, sinking sand. From what I have heard through the grape vine, I'm not alone.

The problem with comparing, envy, or jealousy is there are no winners, for it can lead to either self-loathing or pride. Neither one is desirable, healthy, or God's design for our lives. Not only that, but it also alienates us from joining our hearts with others in pure love. For the Bible tells us clearly in Romans 12:15-16 (TPT) what we are called to do:

"Celebrate with those who celebrate, and weep with those who grieve. Live happily together in a spirit of harmony, and be as mindful of another's worth as you are your own. Don't live with a lofty mindset, thinking you are too important to serve others, but be willing to do menial tasks and identify with those who are humble-minded. Don't be smug or even think for a moment that you know it all."

God's Word is a road map pointing us in the right direction, far removed from any wrong path we might be traveling on at this moment. Shortly, we will unfurl His road map even further and lay out truths to get us moving in the right direction. Even with the best map available, we can be inclined to go off-roading when our eyes turn away from God to ourselves. Then, we get whacked by envy branches, jolted by jealousies potholes, and stuck in the mud of comparison. Thankfully, God's GPS, God's paths are secure and able to reroute us, no matter how many times we take the wrong exit toward our flesh life.

Off-Roading

I was unable to grasp how much God loved me because of comparison. Growing up, I was comparing myself to others constantly, and this became second nature. My self-worth was at bargain-basement prices. With all of that, I had a hard time loving myself. The value I placed on myself was next to nil. My self-esteem had no steam to propel me to a place of ever feeling my worth because I was unable to believe how much God loved me.

The rare times I did feel good about myself were fleeting and few and far between. Somehow, when appearance started to really matter to me, the enemy came peddling his wares like a traveling salesman wearing cheap, intoxicating perfume. He held up his sparky baubles like *Aladdin's* peddler: "Combination hookah [and] coffee maker that also makes julienne fries."

Even though I don't like coffee, I bought it; I bought the lie that took me off God's plan into a tangled mess of deceit. A distortion somewhere brewed that I had to not only be pretty, but the *prettiest.* Ridiculous, it seems, just like all Satan's lies. Our minds see the prize, hear the pitch, and have our wallets out in a blink of an eye. Because it sounds so enticing, we turn a blind eye to God's truth and the fact that what we are buying is broken, flawed, and simply incapable of working. God's truths center us back to wholeness like Psalm 19:7–9 (*MSG*) declares:

"The revelation of God is whole and pulls our lives together.
The signposts of God are clear and point out the right road.
The life-maps of God are right, showing the way to joy.
The directions of God are plain and easy on the eyes.

God's reputation is twenty-four-carat gold, with a lifetime guarantee. The decisions of God are accurate down to the nth degree."

Eviction Notice

Since I, too, was mesmerized by the cool possibility of being the fairest one of them all, I accepted that lie, signing my name to receive it. It made itself at home, kicking back in a recliner, feet propped up, living on easy street with me as an effortless target. But then one day, I got a whiff of its stench of lies and kicked the shady intruder to the curb. The kicking-out process was more of a slow move out of my life though, and the lies had to pick up their trash talk with each step to the curb. And I say, good riddance.

Through all the decades of comparing my looks, talents (or lack thereof), body, skill, etc., it seems easy to compare on so many levels or side by side with the dumbest things. Can I get a witness? Though I can still find my mind veering toward that well-worn path of comparison, I'm backing up and out of it way quicker, hitting fewer potholes and not allowing myself to get stuck spinning my wheels in the enemy's trap.

Recently, while having a heartfelt discussion with the Lord about this nemesis, he dropped a memory in my mind. It was a clue, revealing how at one point in my life this became a foot-in-the-door entry to a legacy of comparison, coupled with my lack of knowing His deep love for me.

Side-By-Side Comparison

There are things in our lives that can cling to us like clothes without a dryer sheet. Whether it is words spoken over us or things we perceive to be truth from our own filtered perceptions, a fun quote to remember is: "Don't believe everything you think" (Allan Lokos).

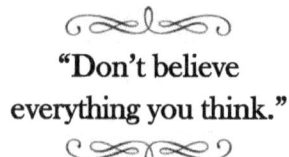
"Don't believe everything you think."

Harmless words spoken with or without any ill will intended can filter through a distorted grid. What I'm about to tell you, I believe, was not to harm me. Sadly, however, it did – all because of my grid.

As you know, I was born on July 17th, and my cousin Lavonna was born only 13 days before me, on the 4th of July. What a fun day to have a birthday!

Both parents and paternal grandparents were no doubt excited to see two new baby girls enter the family so close together. I'm sure Grandma's house was all a buzz and full of laughter, joy filling the home with our first get-together. That special day, during our visit, we were laid side by side on a bed, all dolled up in our cute dresses, picture-perfect!

As I lay next to my petite cousin in comparison, I seemed to resemble a linebacker. Hey, I was in the womb longer, remember? That has got to count for something.

There it was in black and white, clear as day. An untouched glossy photo cannot lie. I was indeed bigger. It is neither here nor there, and yet there were words spoken of how much bigger I was in comparison to my cousin, hurting my mom's feelings, which probably triggered fear in her.

Though she was never heavy, she worried about her weight all her life. I was too young to remember what was spoken over me, yet my mom rehearsed those words that had hurt her many times through the years. It is one thing to share our testimony in a place of healing and freedom to bring others to the same realization. It's another thing to go over hurts that remain unresolved. It's like picking at a scab that is trying to heal, delaying the healing process.

I now realize this one piece of the puzzle is part of the bigger picture of my comparing, competing, and poor body image that seemed unshakable. When I look back at pictures of me as a youth, I cry for the sweet little girl who thought she was fat. Even if I *was* bigger, my worth did not diminish, neither will it ever in God's eyes. God cares about our health and wellbeing, not a number on the scale or pant size. He knit us together in our mother's womb: some taller, shorter, bigger, smaller. He looked at us and said, "It is good." I like to remind myself that weight and age are just numbers. Let's go further and call them lucky ones.

Shiny Objects

A couple of months ago while perusing the Internet, I was drawn in to this beautiful rose gold sparkly tablecloth. Sparkling right next to it, I saw a silver sparkly tablecloth too. Be still, my heart. All that bling distracted me; its hypnotic glitter guided my hands to hit the 'purchase now' button, bypassing reading the details of these items like I normally would.

Overcome by excitement over the glittering newly purchase, I was beyond eager to place them in my window display at Chase Me Again, a quaint thrift store where I used to work.

As I anxiously awaited my package to arrive, I grabbed the mail, gazing at a small package. I thought to myself, *Surely, this cannot be my tablecloths.* Apparently, it could be. You saw it coming, didn't you?

In all the hype of glitter and glamour, I failed to read the fine print. I'm now the proud owner of two nonrefundable, shimmery doilies.

We can easily buy the enemy's glossy images of how we should look, sound, or act. When we feel we don't make the cut, we might feel shortchanged, like a measly doily, instead of a glorious, well-rounded tablecloth.

May we remind ourselves to not buy the lie to compare, for we are not called to be prideful, self-loathing or filled with self-pity, which buries our joy in all of its oppressive falsehoods.

I pray that we are able to learn to love ourselves as God does – passionately and lavishly. He thinks you are perfect. In fact, you're His favorite. That love will spill over into loving others with the same love we have received from our Papa Daddy. That, my friend, calls for a celebration, and if you need a couple of doilies with serious bling for decoration, you know who to call. I will hook you up, and you don't even need to read the fine print.

Aww Nuts

As I write this, I'm watching a blue jay steal walnuts, one by one, from a squirrel house my husband built for two cute squirrels.

Watching this play out, I find myself a tad bit unhappy that Mr. Blue Jay has entered a home that was not built for him. This is how comparison and competing robs us piece by piece; it carries -off the identity of who we are in Christ and the provision He has laid out specially for us. The enemy robs us every time we compare or compete in an unhealthy fashion. It robs our peace, our joy, creativity, and depletes our resources, exhausting us in its empty pursuits.

As Romans 12:15-16 reminded us earlier, not only are we called to rejoice with those who rejoice and weep with those who weep, but do it wholeheartedly. If we cannot, one by one, our gifts, talents, and destiny can get carried away with our nutty comparison, only to be eaten, dropped, or buried by our detrimental thinking and behaviors. Our blue-jay thoughts steal the joy the Lord has for us, leaving us feeling empty. Just as I happily replenished the squirrel house of what was robbed of them, so, too, does God replenish what was taken from us. He will replenish even if it's our own brokenness or someone's wrong choices towards us that makes us feel cheated us out of His love.

> **The enemy robs us of peace, joy, and creativity every time we compare or compete in unhealthy ways.**

Room At The Table

I'm rather surprised at how many times the Lord has brought squirrels into my life to bring a lesson in one form or another. It reminds me of the book *All I Really Need To Know I Learned In Kindergarten* by Robert Fulghum. However, mine would be *All I Really Need To Know I Learned From Squirrels.*

I'm blaming this silliness on pandemic lockdowns. Just the other day, I watched two squirrels fighting for food, chasing each other around the tree trunk over and over again. The thing is, there was plenty of food. Almonds were in the squirrel house, and on the side of the tree was a box feeder filled with peanuts that my friend Bea gave me. Yet, they both insisted to be in the little house. Finally, I decided to place some squirrel food in an empty birdbath and move it closer, hoping for them to stop the madness. Nope! It didn't work. Try as I may, they still fought and refused to delight themselves in the other gifts offered them.

I heard the Lord lovingly say, "My children do that. I have gifts, talents, and callings on their lives, yet they want what others have and miss the joy that comes from variety in My Kingdom. Each person has My glory; there is no need to fight for attention or accolades."

We scramble for the almond in life when we are called to dine on a peanut. And as the saying goes, "There is room for everybody at the table." How boring life would be without the artists, musicians, singers, writers, actors, chefs, dancers, athletes, and so much more! Each one has the potential to bring such beauty and glory to God. What a joyful thing to honor each other's gifting with encouragement and celebration. Variety is the spice of life, and this is one occasion I can handle some extra spice.

"Yes, you are my darling companion. You stand out from all the rest. For the curse of sin surround you, still you remain as pure as a lily, even more than all the others" (Song of Songs 2:2, TPT).

Jesus Loves The Little Children

When we compare or compete in unhealthy ways, we miss out on the fullness of life God gave us and to be the best versions of our God-given selves. Rejoicing with others over their successes never diminishes our value; it increases it, depositing into our heavenly bank account. I'm reminded of a time when I was overlooked for a promotion, and even though I, too, had the experience for the job, my friend was picked over me. I was hurt, and instead of truly rejoicing with her, I nursed a grudge, forgetting to believe that God doesn't make a mistake. I pushed aside His Word that tells us to rejoice with those who rejoice, choosing my own fleshly path.

One day, I said, "God, I don't like being like this." Then, I looked up to a beautiful picture of Jesus on the wall drawn by France and Richard Hook (whose art I absolutely love). They depicted Jesus smiling, surrounded by little children. One child stood in front of Him as His loving hands cupped her face, while all the other children circled around them with love and celebration. No downcast looks of anger for not being the one highlighted. They knew they were in His presence, equally loved and valued.

Right there, I repented of my attitude and continued to bring it to the cross if any impure or unloving thoughts crossed my mind. How freeing and beautiful it is to celebrate God's favor on others. I know how blessed I feel when I see people rejoicing for me from the bottom of their hearts while waiting for His hands to cup their faces. We all have areas we are waiting and contending for; areas where we need Him to bring all His goodness to. His Word promises us He is no respecter of persons, for He truly loves all the little children, and that, my dear friend, includes you.

Jesus knows me, this I love.

Our Secret Garden

The Secret Garden tells us of the story of Mary Lennox, a disagreeable girl with a sour expression, who was sent to Misselthwaite Manor to live with her uncle after her parents died. Before residing at the manor, she had a brief stay at the poor English clergyman's home along with his five children. By her second day, they had already given her a nickname that made her furious. Basil was the first to call her 'Mistress Mary Quite Contrary' as she made heaps of earth and paths for a pretend garden in the clergyman's backyard.

In the same fashion Basil teased his sisters, he danced round her too, singing, "Mistress Mary, quite contrary, how does your garden grow? With silver bells, and cockle shells, and marigolds all in a row."

It was not until her transformation living at the Manor, and digging in the secret garden's dirt with her friend Dickon, that her destiny began to fully blossom. Just like the Lily of the valley and Canterbury bells waking up from their garden beds, pushing back the slumbering soil, eager to burst forth from their once-hidden beauty, so, too, Mary bloomed. Having been drenched in love, she was now flourishing under its tender care. Eyes were yet to see the newfound revelation of what she was truly made for. The taunting that once felt like a curse to Mary catapulted her into a blessing. When she saw her true purpose, it all came into the light. She embraced her God-given talent to now thrive, just like the once closed-up, neglected garden. Those things you once deemed a curse are unfurling into a fragrant garden of overflowing blessing and redemption.

From Our *Whys* to God's Wonders

Destination Known

Here are a few travel tips to steer us away from comparison:

1. Starting Point: "Love the Lord your God with every passion of your heart, with all the energy of your being, and with every thought that is within you.' This is the great and supreme commandment. And the second is like it in importance: 'You must love your friend in the same way you love yourself" (Matthew 22:37-39, TPT).

We were made in God's image. We belong to Papa Daddy, and we are His favorite. No mistakes, no flub-ups, no rejects. When He looked at you, He declared you *very good.* Even those things you do not celebrate or even understand about yourself will one day be diamonds – cut, polished, and brilliant, sparkling multifaceted, and reflecting the Father's light and His radiant image. He has a plan in all of it.

When we love the Lord with every passion and all our energy and being, that leaves little time to compare. That love from God gives us the traction to love ourselves so we can love others.

2. Follow the GPS: Look up verses that will help your journey to overcome comparison. Here are a few locations:

"I'm obviously not trying to flatter you or water down my message to be popular with men, but my supreme passion is to please God. For if all I attempt to do is please people, I would not be the true servant of the Messiah" (Galatians 1:10, TPT).

"Let everyone be devoted to fulfill the work God has given them to do with excellence, and their joy will be in doing what's right and being themselves, and not in being affirmed by others. Every believer is ultimately responsible for his or her own conscience" (Galatians 6:4-5, TPT).

"God's marvelous grace imparts to each one of us varying gifts and ministries that are uniquely ours..." (Romans 12:6, TPT). The Message translation of this verse has it thus: "So since we find ourselves fashioned into all these excellently formed and marvelously functioning parts in Christ's body, let's just go ahead and be what we were made to be, without enviously or pridefully comparing ourselves with each other, or trying to be something we aren't."

"Of course, we wouldn't dare to put ourselves in the same class or compare ourselves with those who rate themselves so highly. They compare themselves to one another and make up their own standards to measure themselves by, and then they judge themselves by their own standards. What self-delusion! But we are those who choose to limit our boasting to only the measure of the work to which God has appointed us—a measure that, by the way, has reached as far as you" (2 Corinthians 10:12-13, TPT).

3. Embrace You: Learn to love the things you thought were your weak areas. Do you feel you talk too much? Maybe, just maybe, you were created to do so. Are you sensitive and get teased about it? It is a gift; celebrate it! Perhaps you think outside the box or color outside the lines; I applaud you! Allow the Lord to help you stop loathing those things and to, instead, start loving the very things God instilled in you for His glory. When our son Trent was little, I would say, "You want Mommy to hold you?" To which he would say, "Mommy, hold you me?" Embrace you so you can embrace others.

4. Walk in Humility: When we struggle with our self-worth, sometimes we might feel a need to promote ourselves in the hopes to elevate our low self-esteem. Those desires, at times, can increase when others share accomplishments that leave you feeling somehow diminished. Our slumping image can lead us to bolster ourselves up in an attempt to convince ourselves and others of our value. When we continue to build our worth on the truth of God's Word and His love for us, those desires to have to prove ourselves to others slowly disappear. The truth is, no matter how loud someone toots their own horn out of their own insecurities, it will never drown out yours. Our position is to stay in a posture of humility. And if our insecurities draw us to toot our own horn, allow the Lord to toot your horn for you. Our job is to make it a priority to honor those around us as we learn to walk in true humility.

1 Peter 5:6 (NIV) is a beautiful reminder: "Humble yourselves, therefore, under God's mighty hand, that he may lift you up in due time." Your Papa Daddy knows how to honor you in the right season.

> *"He paints the lily of the field. He perfumes each lily bell. If He loved the little flowers, I know He loves me well."* —Maria Straus

> *"As we tend our garden, we nourish our souls."* —Anonymous

Be You.

> *"For comparison is the thief of joy."* —Theodore Roosevelt

> *"Whatever you are, be a good one."* —Abraham Lincoln

"And the dandelion does not stop growing because it is told it is a weed. The dandelion does not care what others see. It says, 'One day, they'll be making wishes upon me.'" —B. Atkinson

Whenever we feel the need to go off-roading into comparison or another warbling from the enemy, let's pull out the map of God's Word, tracing the lines to roads that lead to His truth and our healing.

> *"It's no use to going back to yesterday, because I was a different person then."* —Alice in Wonderland

Reclaiming Prayer

Lord Jesus, I thank You for lovingly creating me in Your image. I'm a unique, one-of-a-kind creation, and You are well pleased with me, and I am learning to be pleased with me too.

Chapter 7

Never Enough

The Lord Says You Are Enough

"You perceive every moment of my heart and soul, and you understand my every thought before it even enters my mind."
—Psalm 139:2 (TPT)

Tweedledee And Tweedledum

When I think of *performance* and *perfection,* I liken them to the almost identical twins Tweedledee and Tweedledum from Lewis Carroll's book, *Through the Looking Glass.* These two were good at telling *Alice in Wonderland* a sad story and multiplying it. There actually is a definition of Tweedledee and Tweedledum! It is described as *any two persons or things that differ only slightly from each other* (collinsdictionary.com). The duo, also known as T and T, is an accurate interpretation of how operating in unhealthy performance and perfectionism to gain our self-worth can be extremely explosive and self-destructive.

The underlining factors that can lead us into becoming a Tweedledee (performance-based) or a Tweedledum (perfectionism-based) are at the very core of our being. Without being grounded in the knowledge of God's deep, unconditional love for us, we settle for a counterfeit version of ourselves. People-pleasing will become our number-one priority to save face, cover our shame, and fit in. Our Heavenly Father is the only approval we will ever need.

For most of my life, I have scrounged around in a pigpen rooting for man's approval, squandering my God-given inheritance just like the prodigal son. Fear of man will drive you to places you are not meant to go in your God-given identity. Like the prodigal, we, too, can come to our senses, leaving the smelly pigpen of people-pleasing, performance, and perfectionism, finding our way home to our loving Father who has been waiting for us all along.

Finding Our Way Out

Let's take a closer look at perfectionism, which is defined as *the need to appear or to be perfect, even to believe it is possible to achieve perfection* (goodtherapy.org). Brene Brown, a writer and research professor at Houston Graduate College of Social Work, says, "Perfection is not the same thing as striving to be your best. Perfection is not about healthy achievement and growth." She explains that perfectionism is used by many as a shield to protect against the pain of blame, judgment, or shame. While on the other hand, performance is described as *an act of staging or presenting a play, or other form of entertainment* (languages.oup.com, paraphrased).

As a junior high student, I remember having a group of high school drama students present a skit, and one young man proceeded to lay on the floor and imitate a piece of bacon sizzling in a hot frying pan. My first thought was *you get credit for doing that? Sign me up!* They actually had me at bacon.

Though the world may give us credit for performing and being perfect at it, we are not called to be bacon. Acting out for approval and striving for love buries our God-given individuality, until we lose sight of who we really were created to be. It is hard to swim upstream when our culture strongly applauds performance and perfectionism. It saddened me while doing research on this topic to see that the majority of articles about being performance-driven had a positive spin.

When we feel we need to perform, put on an act, or wear a mask, we build a wall that forbids intimacy (into me, see). For me, letting people see the real me felt too vulnerable, exposed, and fearful that I would be unlovable.

Remember my friend's litmus test in Chapter 3? Who do I want my soul to be naked before? This is an important question to ask when sharing your heart, especially at a tender stage of our healing. If you already know you're in a safe place, with your heart opened wide, let the light of God's love into any dark areas of brokenness and receive your glorious healing.

It is important to guard the pearl of pain that cost us something by not throwing it before people who could trample it. This is especially important during the vulnerable time when starting out our journey of authenticity. The more we open up to safe, loving people, the more the wind of love gathers beneath our wings, taking us from where our story once brought shame to a place where we can soar.

The more we open up to safe, loving people, the more wind of love gathers beneath our wings.

Beautiful transformation can shift us from being a TweedleDOer to a TweedleBEer. The BEer no longer functions out of brokenness' detrimental ways to soothe beastly lies of inferiority, insecurity, and unlovability that once forced us into spiritual barrenness. We now have the wherewithal to shift into God's presence, basking in His unconditional love; a love that does not require conditions to access His throne room of radiant love, grace, and acceptance. That one act of Jesus dying on the cross for all, uttering the words "It is finished," is good enough for me.

Our part is to surrender to that love and accept its blessing that flows freely from Calvary. No longer tied up in works of legalism, we become undone by the power of His chain-breaking love. Where we were once bound by rules, we are now bound by our love and desire to obey God. Shackle-free, we dive fully into God's wonderful grace, swimming unhindered in His wildly delightful joy, celebrating the gift of being ourselves in all our imperfections.

The Martha in me—the TweedleDOer—is now hushed, as my Mary's heart has room to breathe and just TweedleBE (Luke 10:38-42). The bullhorn Martha spoke through, saying, "Don't you think it's unfair that my sister left me to do all the work by myself?" is growing faint, for I have tasted the new wine of liberating truths. It is life-giving wine in new wine skins, as my soul gives God's glory permission to shine through the cracks of my imperfections.

That is the Kingdom the living God has chosen for His sons and daughters. Worth comes from God alone, and once we collide with His radical love, it transforms our lives forever. There, we find acceptance, wholeness, and a desire to seek God, walking in humility, no longer needing a pat on the back or thumbs-up to prop up our faltering ego. We leave our ego at the foot of the cross, perfectly content to hear the applause of only one: our loving Heavenly Father.

Worth comes from God alone.

A 'Tail' Of Two Squirrels

This tale of two squirrels continues from my earlier reference to them in Chapter 6. We named one Fluffernutter, named after our son Trent's concoction made of peanut butter, marshmallow crème, and ingenuity (back when our snack cabinet rivaled Old Mother Hubbard's). Apparently, the fluffernutter sandwich had existed since the early 20th century, whereas all this time, I thought Trent had invented it! The second squirrel, I affectionately named Fluffy because...he is.

When I first saw Fluffy perched on our curly willow, I was giddy. Grabbing a jar of peanuts, I scampered to the tree, squirrel-like, which of course made him scurry up the tree quickly. He clearly knew I was not part of his tribe. Even though I pride myself on having been a squirrel in my sixth-grade play, perhaps my portrayal was not as stellar as I once believed. I conceded having a friendship with this little critter and surrendered my treasure of nuts by throwing them to the ground and heading back into the house. My peace offering of sorts was a tad woeful; I was unable to forge a safe place for my guest to munch. Living in the middle of a pandemic, I became determined to not only feed the birds and squirrels, but I was also hoping to get the squirrels to eat from my hand.

I thought Fluffy might like to know I have squirrel moments too! If he knew I could relate to him, perhaps he might reconsider. It was not long before my frown turned upside down, gleeful to see my provision for him was graciously accepted. Watching my new friend, I saw another squirrel at the edge of our property darting back and forth, digging and looking and digging some more. Through the kitchen window, I encouraged Fluffernutter to come closer. "Don't work so hard – all you need is right here!" I coached her through the closed window.

Suddenly, it dawned on me that Fluffernutter was quite a bit like me, scrappy at times, rather frantic at others, driven by an insatiable desire to try to figure everything out independently. Foraging for approval, scrounging for praise, seeking love that was tenacious in its unconditionality, the gnawing void forbade my soul to fully enter the rest that God's love provided.

By this time, I was fully invested in seeing Fluffernutter come to a place of peace, and eventually, that day, she did. She not only found the plentiful source for her supply, but she also found the gentle rhythm of provision and peace she could trust in. So, too, I'm learning that my one true source of provision is in Jesus, for His love and acceptance replaces the emptiness that performance and perfection had to offer.

My newfound friend and kindred spirit perhaps felt what Anne of Green Gables did with her bosom buddy Dianna Barry. Miss Fluffernutter now comes up to our French doors as a daily honored guest. Peering in while dining on a hearty pecan, we share a moment of solidarity whenever we can. Occasionally sitting on the floor, I peek out at her with joy and camaraderie as we do a toast with our pecans through the glass panes. It's as if she is saying, "Freedom has never tasted so good!" I so hear you, girlfriend.

The Five-Year-Old Itch

My maternal grandmother loved to sing, and when my mom and her sister were younger, she signed them up to perform on KGON radio. By the time I was in high school, KGON became a rock station. It was a lot of fun telling classmates my mom once sang on that legendary station. They not only sang on KGON, but also for a radio show called "Stars of Tomorrow," along with countless other gigs.

Recently, our son Derek posted one of their records, *The Whitehead Sisters—Infantry Song*. It was special to hear them sing, even though they sound like Alvin and the Chipmunks due to the record's quality and age. It warmed my heart to hear my mom sing.

Since my Grandma Alice's love for singing did not go away, when I was five, she hooked me up to my first singing performance of "Jesus Loves Me" at the Grand Ole Minthorne Church in Milwaukie, Oregon. My mom made me an adorable red with white polka-dotted Swiss dress for my big debut. As cute and laborious as the dress was for mom to make, that thing made me itch...something terrible. Trying to perform my song with itches screaming for attention was not an easy feat. Thankfully, there was no rousing demand for an encore, with the congregation holding up Zippo lighters, their flames beckoning to belt out another tune. I was able to scratch away like I had just landed smack dab on top of a fire-ant colony as soon as I left the stage.

Performance and perfection can seem like innocent ways to get attention, love, or approval. Yet, they will never satisfy, and even though they produce a lot of misery, we still can feel the need that the show must go on and on and on. While keeping up appearances when we are struggling, the cloak of shame is itching to come off. I'm singing "Jesus Loves Me" when I am not sure He really can love me...*all* of me - my pain, my sins, and a sea of regrets. And yet, thankfully, He does. What joy, what peace!

Get Off The Hamster Wheel

The other day, I found myself in full-blown hamster wheel mode, spinning out of sheer habit while engrossed in a project. The all too familiar spinning feverishly for two fruitless endeavors of performance and perfection! A squeaky wheel longing for oil of approval, love, and acceptance becomes a grueling taskmaster with an insatiable appetite.

My husband calls this lie the *if'en factor*. If I do, then I am good; if I don't, then I'm bad. That is not how God loves us, for His love is not based on our performance.

"But God shows his love for us that while we were still sinners, Christ died for us" (Romans 5:8, ESV).

There is nothing wrong with wanting to do a job well or to pursue excellence. But no one should measure your worth or value without God's redeeming love for you in the equation. God created you and said you were good without meeting any quota. Our motivation should be learning how to receive God's love more completely and love Him back, leaving works and perfectionism out of the equation.

Leave works and perfectionism out of the equation.

"And God saw everything that He had made, and behold, it was very good (suitable, pleasant) and He approved it completely. And there was evening and there was morning, a sixth day" (Genesis 1:31, AMPC).

When God created Adam, he simply asked Adam to use his God-given creativity to name all the living creatures. Then, seeing it was not good for man to be alone, He created Eve. Their mission, if they chose to accept it, was to enjoy the beauty of the garden, drinking up the moments in all their beautiful sights, tranquil sounds, heady fragrances, and jaw-dropping wonder. Most importantly, drawing joy from their magnificent loving Creator carried the most intoxicating fragrance of all. Even surrounded by love and beauty, the call to rest without toil was short-lived. For "the serpent was more subtle and crafty than any living creature of the field which the Lord God had made" (Genesis 3:1, AMPC).

Dictionary.com defines subtle as *delicate in meaning or intent, difficult to perceive or understand*. The first humans crossed that artful, fine-drawn line by the crafty enemy, bringing them to a place that would no longer be Paradise. They became caught in a delicate, yet powerful web of deceit spun masterfully by the father of all lies. Silken threads of doubt were woven in, questioning God's love and His promises of rest and provision. Enticed by the snake charmer, Eve bit into a lie and handed it to Adam, who did the same, instantly making their mission seem quite impossible.

Understanding the enemy is quite indistinct and rather tricky. It is important to put on the armor of God every day to withstand the enemy's attacks.

The Wildest Ride In The Wilderness

No amount of craving unhealthy kudos or accolades is ever worth the toll it took to get them. Like sand slipping through our fingers, they are gone, leaving us empty-handed once again. It is a never-ending vicious circle.

Once we ask the Holy Spirit to help us heal our need to perform and to root out perfectionism, He will gladly do it. He knows how crippling our walk becomes with such encumberment. It is a journey of relinquishing our old ways of coping into fresh ways of approaching life.

Since a child, my core mathematical equation of love was: performance adds up to love; perfect equals even more love. That super-sized lie needed a super-sized crowbar of God's love to pry it out of me. My heart's prayer is for us to grasp these truths to put us on the right track of healing. If I was to compare my healing track to a Disney World ride, though, I would love it if it was the 60-mph-in-under-three-seconds Rock 'n' Roller Coaster in Disney's Hollywood Studios. A G-force of trajectory and speed right into my fast-track healing would be preferable. Although I have experienced speedy deliverances, of which I'm always a fan, God usually chooses the Tomorrowland Transit Authority People Mover instead: a slow-moving process, coming from the confessions of a spiritual lead foot. Maybe you can relate?

I'm more than ready to speed things up and get things moving quickly. Yet, God will at times use the slow lane toward healing so we can enjoy the journey rather than race to the destination. For in that process, we find humility, our need for community, and relationships that simply cannot happen while we are going full bore to our landing place of liberation.

The majority of my spiritual journeys have not come close to a Dale Earnhardt-style, pedal-to-the-medal finish line, but rather dawdling down the road like a Sunday driver. Yet, in all the winding through those country roads, I have found God's love through the love of family, friends, and even strangers. Through this, I gained more grace and patience as I waited upon the Lord. We can trust God, whatever lane He chooses to get us to our final destination. His Word promises, "He has made everything beautiful in its time" (Eccelesiates 3:11, NIV).

We can trust God to get us to our destination.

If by chance you get on the fast track, remember the following instructions from our family's favorite ride, Big Thunder Mountain in Disneyland: as you zip through the mountainous terrain to your healing, "Hold on to your hats, folks, 'cause this is the wildest ride in the wilderness." Can I get a yeehaw and an amen?

Brought To You By The Letter P... Prince of Peace

"You will guard me and keep me in perfect and constant **peace** whose mind [both its inclination and its character] is stayed on You, because he commits himself to You, leans on You, and hopes confidently in You. So trust in the Lord (commit yourself to Him, lean on Him, hope confidently in Him) forever; for the Lord God is an everlasting Rock [the Rock of Ages] . . . Lord, You will ordain **peace** (God's favor and blessings, both temporal and spiritual) for us, for You have also wrought in us and for us all our work" (Isaiah 26: 3, 4, 12, AMPC).

Spiritual Warfare

"In conclusion, be strong in the Lord [be empowered through your union with Him]; draw your strength from Him [that strength which His boundless might provides].

"Put on God's whole armor [the armor of a heavy-armed soldier which God supplies], that you may be able successfully to stand up against [all] the strategies and the deceits of the devil. For we are not wrestling with flesh and blood [contending only with physical opponents], but against the despotisms, against the powers, against [the master spirits who are] the world rulers of this present darkness, against the spirit forces of wickedness in the heavenly (supernatural) sphere.

"Therefore, put on God's complete armor, that you may be able to resist and stand your ground on the evil day [of danger], and, having done all [the crisis demands], to stand [firmly in your place].

"Stand therefore [hold your ground], having tightened the **belt of truth** around your loins and having put on **the breastplate of integrity** and of moral rectitude and right standing with God,

"And having **shod your feet** in preparation [to face the enemy with the firm-footed stability, the promptness, and the readiness produced by the good news] of the Gospel of peace" (Ephesians 6:10, AMPC).

Shod Your Beautiful Feet

"How beautiful upon the mountains are the feet of him who brings good tidings, who publishes peace, who brings good tidings of good, who publishes salvation, who says to Zion, Your God reigns!" (Isaiah 52:7, AMPC).

Satan loves to whisper in our ears that God is not enough, and since we are made in His image, we are certainly not enough. We end up striving for love and acceptance in all the wrong places, hopping on a people-pleasing wagon to find our self-worth and identity.

God's Got It

One day, when our son Derek was around two years old, he was playing with his Hot Wheels car on the brown shag carpet in our apartment, complete with blazing orange kitchen counter Formica too. At that time, I thought *The Brady Bunch* called, wanting their interior design back! Lying on that plush dreamy shag, I watched Derek play with his little car. My heart was full of such joy for that little guy, and no undesirable funky carpet or counter tops would rob me of that.

All of a sudden, I heard Derek say, "Oh no! My wheel is gone!" Then he said a precious simple prayer, "Jesus, help me find my wheel." I sprung up into action, combing the lush brown carpet like blades of dried-up grass, determined to rise up victorious just like my mom who always prayed and always found things. I was convinced she and God had a special agreement that I was not privy to. Pulling my fallen hair away from my face, I was laser-focused to find the microscopic wheel that went AWOL when Derek said sweetly, "I'll just let Jesus find it."

How precious is that? That's how I want to live my life – with simple trust for the big things as well as the little ones. And while our wheels spin with performance and perfection in a vicious cycle, we can trust God to help us to make it right, turning our wheel spins of compulsion into joy and recreation as He intended.

Jesus, take the insane hamster wheel!

Let's quickly ditch the insane hamster wheel that takes us nowhere. Jesus, take the hamster wheel 'cause I can't do it on my own! Won't you sing with me?

The Promise Of Rest

"And so this is still a live promise. It wasn't canceled at the time of Joshua; otherwise, God wouldn't keep renewing the appointment for 'today.' The promise of 'arrival' and 'rest' is still there for God's people. God himself is at rest. And at the end of the journey we'll surely rest with God. So let's keep at it and eventually arrive at the place of rest, not drop out through some sort of disobedience. God means what he says. What he says goes. His powerful Word is sharp as a surgeon's scalpel, cutting through everything, whether doubt or defense, laying us open to listen and obey. Nothing and no one can resist God's Word. We can't get away from it—

no matter what. Now that we know what we have—Jesus, this great High Priest with ready access to God—let's not let it slip through our fingers. We don't have a priest who is out of touch with our reality. He's been through weakness and testing, experienced it all—all but the sin. So let's walk right up to him and get what he is so ready to give. Take the mercy, accept the help" (Hebrews 4:8-16, MSG).

From Our *Whys* To God's Wonder

Wheel of Fortune

List areas you know you struggle with in performing.

_____
_____
_____

Write some ways in which you strive for perfection.

_____
_____
_____

Ask the Lord for the keys to freedom in these areas.

> *"Be free from pride-filled opinions, for they will only harm your cherished unity. Don't allow self-promotion to hide in your hearts, but in authentic humility put others first and view others as more important than yourselves. Abandon every display of selfishness. Possess a greater concern for what matters to others instead of your own interests. And consider the example that Jesus, the Anointed One, has set before us. Let his mindset become your motivation."* —Philippians 2:3-5, TPT

Transform, not perform; reform, not conform.

Reclaiming Prayer

Jesus, we come before You, releasing a need to perform for love or be perfect to receive it. This is a lie from the enemy of our soul, and we renounce it. We ask forgiveness for holding onto idols of performance and perfectionism to earn approval from others and You. Your love surrounds us, filling us to overflowing so we can freely love as You do. Thank You, Jesus. Today, I declare victory.

Chapter 8

Shame On You

The Lord Removes Your Shame

"You saw who you created me to be before I became me!"
—Psalm 139:16 (TPT)

Dressed In Fig Leaves

Growing up in the 60s, saying "shame on you" was as popular as canned spam and Swansons Frozen TV dinners. Fortunately, it became evident as time went on that using asbestos-lined potholders and saying "shame on you" were not good ideas. Who knew? Shame is more toxic than asbestos and packs a wallop that can knock you not only into next week but reeling into months or even years, depending on the severity.

Doing research on shame feels like looking at a multi-layered rubber-band ball. One stretches over another, insulating a core belief: "You are bad!" With all the complexities of shame, it could hands-down beat the largest rubber band ball's record, which weighed a whopping 9,032 pounds and used 700,000 rubber bands according to the 2008 *Guinness Book Of World Records.*

Revisiting the fall of Adam and Eve, we see they hid from God, driven by shame after eating the fruit from the tree of knowledge of good and evil. Though God gave them only one restriction, one crafty serpent knew how to capitalize on it, painting a picture with bold, broad, deceitful strokes that God could not be trusted. "Could He really love you," he hissed, "and deny you such goodness at the same time? Surely, that cannot be so!"

Perhaps it is similar to Kaa's hypnotic eyes that seduced Mowgli the man-cub in the *Jungle Book* tale. Like a quick snap of the fingers that led to sin, the instant "Oh snap!" realization of eyes now wide open revealed their nakedness. One bite, one forbidden fruit, by one man and one woman beguiled by one subtle serpent, led to a battle that could now only be won by one sacrificial Lamb.

Shame began to spread its black, inky darkness, muddying the waters of God's love and pure goodness the moment sin entered the door of doubt. So much so, Adam and Eve wasted no time covering their nakedness as their hearts beat wildly in fear of exposure.

> **When feeling ashamed, we naturally want to hide.**

Shame forced them into hiding from love and true intimacy. Its darkness cannot handle the light of transparency or authenticity. Unhealthy secrecy is the calling card of shame. Our natural inclination when carrying shame is to hide under flimsy hand-sewn fig leaves of insecurities. God wants nothing more than to commune with us in the cool of the day just like He desired with Adam and Eve. He knows our fears and needs, and He longs to provide a love covering for His children in whatever state we find ourselves.

The Garden Of Weeden

Shame's message is "I am bad," while guilt's message is "I did something bad" (per Ed Welch, *Shame Interrupted*, 2012). To feel *you* are bad makes the road to healing steeper, grittier, and harder to shake than *I did something bad.* Yet, with the Lord's help, we are more than conquerors in both scenarios. If you believe you're bad to the core of your being, you feel as if you have nowhere to go, for wherever you go, there you are with your so-called bad self. Wrapping lie upon lie, it's just like how the rubber band ball masks your foundational belief that you are bad at the very center of your being.

Abuse is a common breeding ground for shame, and it has been said that the victim of sexual assault can feel more shame than the perpetrator. Innocence is stifled with the weight of others' sins. You have validity for the wounds you have carried, and remember, the abuse was never your fault, no matter what the enemy whispers in your ear.

Something Is Rotten In Denmark

Growing up, I remember two occasions that brought uncomfortable awareness that what I was experiencing was not normal. As mentioned earlier, I was holding repressed memories and memories I never filed as abuse in my mind until well into adulthood.

One day, when I was around five years old, I remember sitting on the couch next to my grandpa. Having a desire to sit on his lap, I inched my way up and found a welcoming spot. After my grandparents left, my mom scolded me for trying to sit on his lap. Fear welled up in me, as my face became hot with embarrassment. Shame opened the door even wider, cozying up to make itself right at home. What I thought was normal behavior suddenly felt dirty, my emotions topsy-turvy with this unsettling revelation. Newfound fears and shame applauded even louder, as they were now ushered to the front-row seat of my thinking. My world was upside down and inside out, confusing what was a normal, appropriate touch with what was not.

Though I'm sure my mom's intentions were to warn me solely out of concern, it came across that she was angry. Anger can be fear-based, which causes an inability to communicate in a more loving manner. Coupled with shame as a method to promote obedience, it became a chunk of rubble that buried my joy and childlike freedom.

What started filtering through my tender grid and laid a sturdy foundation was the thought *I'm bad.* As it carried through my adult life, my friend Donna calls me 'tenderoni,' which reminds me of pasta. Emotionally, at times, I have gone beyond the al dente stage, feeling overcooked and soggy. My personality for the most part is to be a rule-follower and people-pleaser, so to do something wrong was heartbreaking. Looking back, I have wondered if my mom experienced sexual abuse from the tell-tale signs she carried. If not, the verbal and emotional abuse she described that she suffered from her family can also produce similar fruit as sexual abuse.

Who's The Boss's Son?

The second occasion was when I was 12, navigating being a pre-pubescent tween and feeling all the awkwardness that comes with it. My dad's boss had a son in his twenties who would visit our family. I liked seeing him, for he paid attention to me. One time, I sat next to him, enjoying his company. After he left, my mom told me not to do that again. That same panicky feeling that rose within me at age five came flooding back. Suddenly, from that moment on, I felt fearful of him. I'm thankful my mom saw a red flag and warned me of it, but this time around, I was not feeling shame but full-blown fear.

The problem with being sexually abused as a child is your compass to navigate life malfunctions, due to external influences that God never intended. You cannot process things the same as a child who was not abused. Your thoughts become rewired for survival, self-preservation coated in fear and twisted with shame. You learn to try to read people's thoughts and actions: trying to stay one step ahead of them so you do not become a victim becomes an art. In your brokenness, you cannot judge healthy relationships, falling back into choosing people who devalue you, because, for one, you do not value yourself, and it's familiar to you. Not only that, as you grow older in this depraved state, you miss out on the giddy feelings of what it's like to have your hand held or kiss a boy for the first time and all the other firsts that were distorted and robbed from you.

One night, this young man came over to our house while I was swimming in our pool. He hung around the pool, chatting with my dad as I waited for my getaway. My skin turning into a Sunsweet prune finally propelled me up the ladder, and I dashed to the shower upstairs in my parents' room. I kept checking out their bedroom window to view the pool and his whereabouts, which was still poolside. I rushed to my room, biding my time until he left, my heart racing with fear.

While trying to distract myself as my wet hair slowly dried, I heard my bedroom door open, and he slowly walked in, knelt in front of me, lifted my chin, and kissed me. The fear was racing through me, and I felt not only dirty but helpless. To be completely honest, I wrestled with calling this sexual abuse when I first started recalling all the abuse that touched my body uninvited. It seemed trivial, barely registering compared to the other acts that were more touchy and depraved.

The truth is, any unwelcome act is abuse. And as I mentioned earlier, one touch is too much. It is important to see it as such so you can let go and forgive. If you don't think it's a sin against you, then you see no reason to forgive, which is crucial for forward healing. I'm so thankful for my mom's radar and for watching over me. Countless times, she warned me of danger when I was unaware of it. Her faith and love for God and family helped me through a very dark time, even when she was unaware of so many of them. Her prayers were a lifeline and warm hugs of comfort and hope. I miss her love and intercession on my behalf.

If you don't think it's a sin against you, then you see no reason to forgive.

Sadly, I could never tell her about my dad's sexual abuse toward me after his death. I worried not only for her wellbeing, but also, my role as a rescuer was still in tip-top shape. I also knew my mom struggled to fully let go of unforgiveness, and her knowledge of my abuse would hinder my forward movement into freedom.

A Strong Core

I'm so thankful God's Word promises to heal the very core of our brokenness. Here are a few of my favorites:

"Fear not, for you shall not be ashamed; neither be confounded and depressed, for you shall not be put to shame. For you shall forget the shame of your youth..." (Isaiah 54:4, AMPC).

"...now salvation and power are set in place, and the kingdom reign of our God and the ruling authority of his Anointed One are established. For the accuser of our brothers and sisters, who relentlessly accused them day and night before our God, has now been defeated—cast out once and for all. They conquered him completely through the blood of the Lamb and the powerful word of his testimony" (Revelation 12:10-11, TPT).

"And the ransomed of the Lord shall return, and come to Zion with songs and everlasting joy upon their heads: they shall obtain joy and gladness and sorrow and sighing shall flee away" (Isaiah 35:10, KJV).

High School, Low School

Times spent for me in high school had highs and lows. Starting as a freshman, I vowed I would not drink, smoke or do drugs. "A funny thing happened on the way to the theater" was frequently uttered by vaudeville comedians and seemed to perfectly fit my high school years that appeared both as a comedy and tragedy.

Approval of men was at a fever pitch, and my faith muscles developed atrophy not walking with God as I should have been. The truth is, looking for the approval of others will get you nowhere fast. I have walked that dead-end road enough times to become an expert at it. Straddling the fence with our faith is neither healthy nor productive.

Not wanting to feel left out of going to my first high school dance, when I got asked by a well-known high school drug user, I said yes. The idol of approval of man I used to cover shame overshadowed God's will and purpose for my life. It did not take long for him to dump me shortly after that, shattering my already minuscule self-worth into a billion microscopic pieces.

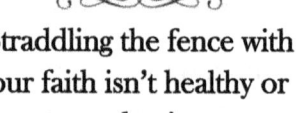

Straddling the fence with our faith isn't healthy or productive.

To him, I was the church lady, and he was the equivalent of Cheech or Chong. Though he voiced admiration for my stand in not drinking or doing drugs, I was no longer dateable. That rejection tore into my fragile ego so much, that not even his pat on the back of admiration toward me was enough. (My God-given identity was MIA.) So, that one drop of approval fuel could not get me to the proper finish line. And since I chose not to fill up with God's love and His approval, I quickly switched lanes right into the fast one.

Soon, God appeared smaller, and the world's ways appeared bigger. I should have seen it coming with dating someone I should not have dated in the first place. But when your identity has been stolen by the enemy, you lose sight of the you God created in the first place.

Drinking became the cool thing to do for my stamp of approval. I hated both the taste and smell; however, the freedom of doing and saying things without the restrictions or insecurities kept me going back for more. Lampshade hats are highly overrated, and so is the stark reality of drinking for acceptance to fit in or numb the pain. The pain will greet you anyway just like that throbbing headache courtesy of a hangover the next morning.

Not only did I begin to drink, but I also took up smoking too, because what on earth does one do with the other hand? Being so cool with your drink in one, you just have to do something cool with the other. Lord have mercy! Such lies the enemy sells us.

There were tell-tale signs I was not made for that lifestyle, for I was afraid to light a match because I might get burned. I plugged my nose while drinking a lot of times because I loathed the taste. How cool is that? Yep, the so-called cool factor went straight out the window, and I said good riddance to it. By the time I was 21 years old, I quit all of that, because I realized to be really cool is to love Jesus with all your heart, soul, and mind and to love others as yourself.

Life will never get better than that truth. No pill, drink, new outfit, promotion, dream vacation, or weight loss will hold a candle to that. By the way, I can now light with a match all by myself. Cool, right?

Singed Souls

When my brother was a teenager, his neighborhood friend Charlie would hang out at our house, and inevitably, something would happen to him. It seemed our dog Herbie loved to pee on his jacket whenever he would lay it on the grass. One day, he was hanging around my dad's trusty Webber grill as he prepared some BBQ. Flames were dancing from the generous Kingsford charcoal lighter fluid dad doused the coals with. Charlie (as most boys I know, including ours) was hypnotized by the flames. Charlie was no exception, for it beckoned him to blow on it in a trance-like manner.

My dad, knowing Charlie's propensity to mishaps, said, "Don't blow on that. It will singe your hair." It was too late. The flames were too powerful to resist, and Charlie's last blow confirmed this sad truth. Raising his face from the hardy blow revealed his singed eyebrows, eyelashes, and pride. I think the red face was not just the work of the flames but also the working of his embarrassment.

Even if we lit the flame ourselves, we serve a good God who promises to bring beauty from the ashes.

There are times when we get too close to a fire, and we feel the heat. We play with matches, thinking we will not get burned (unless you were me in regard to lighting matches), though the warnings tell us otherwise. What I'm about to share is about walking into a place I knew I should not be, yet I blew into it anyway, never once thinking I could get hurt.

Our life choices have consequences that can result in good or not so good. We cannot escape the chain reaction of our choices any more than we can elude gravity's pull. God's Word also tells us, "He makes the sun to rise on the wicked and the good, and makes the rain fall upon the upright and the wrongdoers alike" (Matthew 5:45, AMPC). This two-sided coin tells us not all bad things that happen to us are the product of us making a wrong choice. We live in a fallen world, and that impacts everyone who inhabits it. However, we serve a good and merciful God who promises to bring beauty from the ashes, regardless of whether we are the ones who lit the match and fanned the flames, blowing into it or not.

What's A Nice Girl Like You Doing In A Place Like This?

I remember it like yesterday, down to the outfit. That part seems normal for a girl to recall such a thing. The plan was set: a senior year winter break party at my childhood friend Janet's house (you know the stately long-legged beauty) just down the street while her parents were out of town. Maybe that weekend they were staying at their home away from home by the Trask River. That frequent hangout gathered many, including a handful of our neighbors calling themselves The Trask River Rats, and they always had stories to tell. It was the happening crowd that just so happened to be out of town.

That night, the parties we went to were hopping, the music was blaring, and we were sowing our wild oats like mad farmer girls. The longer the night wore on, the more alcohol I consumed, until finally, at Janet's home, I went downstairs to pray to the porcelain gods. I do not remember any more until I woke up unclothed and watched a figure start to walk out the door. That figure was the brother of a friend who was at our weekend girls' get-together. I yelled at him in total shock over what he had done to me in my drunken state.

At the time, I was dating my high school boyfriend and had made a vow I would not have sex with him or anyone again until after I was married, for I had lost my virginity at 15 to a very persuasive and rather arrogant previous boyfriend. It was one of the worst decisions of my life and happened at the same time my dad was suffering a nervous breakdown. I felt very alone and confused. If I could tell a younger me to save myself for marriage, I would do it in a heartbeat. I'm so thankful to God who covers all our mistakes. What a comfort to know His love covers all.

That night, my heart was beyond sickened by the reality that this act of violence done to my body was irreversible. Adrenaline pumping my body, I quickly got dressed to run up the stairs to tell my friends the trauma that had just occurred. The next day, I could not shower off how dirty I felt or how violated this person's transgression made me feel. To this day, my love for words and describing things cannot fully express these feelings, for they seem indescribable.

The rest of my senior year was like *Dawn of the Living Dead*. I went through the motions, while the bulk of classmates were oblivious to a respected classmate's abhorrent behavior. He flew under the radar of punishment while I was sucked in, mercilessly thrashed around it, and spit out by it. Adding to this weight was never being able to tell my parents about being sexually assaulted because I thought it was my fault. Not having an adult's covering left me feeling alone, with no advocate standing in my corner defending me. Though my mom could tell something was wrong, I did not have the heart to tell her what it was. It was a secret that seemed to never be vindicated, neither was justice served.

I felt he got away with murder, for something died in me that night that took years for God to resurrect and redirect to total redemption. For years, I struggled in the depths of my broken and shattered soul because I felt responsible. If only I stayed home, did not drink, etc. One day, it dawned on me; although I did drink, which I should not have, I was going to a house of girls in the safety of giggles and girl talk and not to be taken advantage of.

It took me years with the Lord's help and love of others to unpack the truth of that dreadful night...that it was never my fault, ever. Though that person apologized after the event, it was a long, bumpy road before I arrived at true forgiveness. I've realized along the way that once a person has been abused by another human in any way, shape, or form, only God can truly heal such brokenness. I hope and pray he has found the freedom and peace God longs to give him.

You Are Virtuous

Please, beloved child, don't blame yourself for your abuse. It is not your fault! Recently, I went up for prayer to cover any residual effects of my sexual abuses, and a woman named Andrea prayed a beautiful prayer over me that I hold near and dear to my heart. As I briefly explained some abuse for her to get a reference, she looked at my tear-streaked face and said, "You are a virtuous woman." She said so, even when I had told her the wrong choices I had made in my past because of the impact of abuses in my life. She once again looked into my eyes, holding my hands, and said so sweetly, "You are a virtuous woman."

YOU are a virtuous woman!

I'm tearing up now, not just for me but for you. YOU are a virtuous woman! Grab ahold of that truth and run like the wind with it. Let it take flight in your spirit and soar. For you were made to soar. (Let Proverbs 31 settle into your spirit and redefine who you are as Christ's radiant bride, for you are...)

A Proverbs 31 Woman

The Radiant Bride

"Who could ever find a wife like this one—she is a woman of strength and mighty valor! She's full of wealth and wisdom. The price paid for her was greater than many jewels Her husband has entrusted his heart to her for she brings him the rich spoils of victory. All throughout her life she brings him what is good and not evil. She searches out continually to possess that which is pure and righteous. She delights in the work of her hands. She gives out revelation-truth to feed others. She is like a trading ship bringing divine supplies from the merchant. Even in the night season she arises and sets food on the table for hungry ones in her house and for others. She sets her heart upon a nation and takes it as her own, carrying it within her. She labors there to plant the living vines. She wraps herself in strength might, and power in all her works. She tastes and experiences a better substance, and her shining light will not be extinguished, no matter how dark the night. She stretches out her hands to help the needy and she lays hold of the wheels of government. She is known by her extravagant generosity to the poor, for she always reaches out her hands to those in need. She is not afraid of tribulation, for all her household is covered in the dual garments of righteousness and grace. Her clothing is beautifully knit together—a purple gown of exquisite linen. Her husband is famous and admired by all, sitting as the venerable judge of his people. Even her works of righteousness she does for the benefit of her enemies. Bold power and glorious majesty are wrapped around her as she laughs with joy over the latter days. teachings are filled with wisdom and kindness as loving instruction pours from her lips. She watches over the ways of her household and meets every need they have. Her sons and daughters arise in one accord to extol her virtues, and her husband arises to speak of her in glowing terms. 'There are many valiant and noble ones, but you have ascended above them all!' Charm can be misleading, and beauty is vain and so quickly fades, but this virtuous woman lives in the wonder, awe, and fear of the Lord. She will be praised throughout eternity. So go ahead and give her the credit that is due, for she has become a radiant woman and all her loving works of righteousness deserve to be admired at the gateways of every city!" (Proverbs 31:1-31, TPT).

Blossoming Like A Rose

Allow those words from your Daddy to cascade over you, washing away anything that would tell you otherwise. You, my beloved sons and daughters, are rising from the ashes like a Phoenix, washed by the blood of the Lamb and the word of your testimony, and may you experience the glorious promise of Isaiah 35:1-10: any dry, barren ground of shame you might carry will soon flow with life-giving water and blossom like a sweet-smelling rose.

"The wilderness and the dry land shall be glad; the desert shall rejoice and blossom like the rose and the autumn crocus. It shall blossom abundantly and rejoice even with joy and singing. The glory of Lebanon shall be given to it, the excellency of [Mount] Carmel and [the plain] of Sharon. They shall see the glory of the Lord, the majesty and splendor and excellency of our God. Strengthen the weak hands and make firm the feeble and tottering knees. Say to those who are of a fearful and hasty heart, Be strong, fear not! Behold, your God will come with vengeance; with the recompense of God He will come and save you. Then the eyes of the blind shall be opened, and the ears of the deaf shall be unstopped. Then shall the lame man leap like a hart, and the tongue of the dumb shall sing for joy. For waters shall break forth in the wilderness and streams in the desert. And the burning sand and the mirage shall become a pool, and the and the thirsty ground springs of water; in the haunt of jackals, where they lay resting, shall be grass with reeds and rushes. And a highway shall be there, and a way; and it shall be called the Holy Way. The unclean shall not pass over it, but it shall be for the redeemed; the wayfaring men, yes, the simple ones and fools, shall not err in it and lose their way. No lion shall be there, nor shall any ravenous beast come up on it; they shall not be found there. But the redeemed shall walk on it. And the ransomed of the Lord shall return and come to Zion with singing, and everlasting joy shall be upon their heads; they shall obtain joy and gladness, and sorrow and sighing shall flee away" (Isaiah 35:1-10, AMPC).

Meet Me At The Tomb

One day, Michelle and I were having a deep conversation about which Mary was at the tomb. There are several Marys in Jesus' life. Michelle has a way of making me want to dig deeper to find the rich treasure of wisdom buried beneath the surface. Dusting off this familiar scripture with fresh eyes, I pondered the Mary Jesus graciously allowed first to witness His glory.

This Mary, the one possessed by seven demons, strikes a chord in me when I think of my sexual abuse encounters. Each violation simultaneously left an imprint of evil while stealing a part of me. It's like a crime scene where incriminating fingerprints smudged my soul.

For quite some time, I did not count some events as abuse – like my dad's boss' son, which is technically considered abuse. Retrieving it from under the rug of shame I had swept it under, I came face to face with its much-needed forgiveness like all the others. However, Mary acquired seven demons during her traumas; we know it could not have been a cakewalk. She had to have suffered tremendously being tag-teamed both emotionally and psychologically with torment and lies so thick even a knife could not cut through them.

Thank God we have a gateway to freedom: "...I speak to you eternal truth: I am the Gate for the flock. All those who broke in before me are thieves who came to steal, but the sheep never listened to them. I am the Gateway.

To enter through me is to experience life, freedom, and satisfaction. A thief has only one thing in mind—he wants to steal, slaughter, and destroy. But I have come to give you everything in abundance, more than you expect—life in its fullness until you overflow" (John 10:7-10, TPT).

> **"I am the Gateway. To enter through me is to experience life, freedom, and satisfaction."**

There is a connection I feel with Mary, for Jesus delivered her from all the trauma that tormented her soul and the shame that came with it. This same freedom rescued me and can rescue you too. His redemptive grace and healing is the same yesterday, today, and forever. He is no respecter of persons - all are welcome to the overflowing banqueting table of His mercy and divine healing.

"He has brought me to his banqueting place, and his banner over me is love [waving overhead to protect and comfort me]" (Song of Solomon 2:4, AMPC).

Lessons Learned From Mary

Here are some things I would like to highlight from John Chapter 20:

1. She was the first to see the tomb empty and the first to see Jesus when He resurrected.

2. "Why are you crying?" Good news was unveiling before her eyes, yet the veil was still dim. Those promises given, which she drank in with every drop, seemed to have died with Jesus. When our faith gets *shaken, not stirred*, don't we, at times, question it? Or am I the only one?

3. "Who are you looking for?" When our faith slides on icy doubts, our first thought might me to overly correct the doubtful situation in our strength when it feels like it has spun out of control. I know, for me, my eyes can look at the situation rather than His face that holds all the hope and does not disappoint.

4. She mistook Him for the gardener: How fitting He would look like a gardener! God's redemption from the fall of Adam and Eve started with a Gardener transforming the garden once cursed by sin and death to teem with abundant, eternal life.

5. She called Him Teacher: I need to remember to slow down, sit at Jesus's feet to listen to Him, and learn to soak in His presence. He is talking to us all the time, even when we don't perceive it. He wants to walk with us and work through us to become a new creature in Christ Jesus, the old passing away to behold the new.

6. Jesus made His 'firsts' to a woman, which was not culturally appropriate then, for women were viewed as second-class citizens with little regard or value. But she was a woman who was delivered from seven demons, no less! He places honor when the world sees little. His nail-scarred hands and feet are His love language declaring your significance.

"You empower me for victory with your wrap-around presence. Your power within makes me strong to subdue, and by stooping down in gentleness you strengthened me and made me great! You've set me free from captivity and now I'm standing complete, ready to fight some more!" (Psalms 18:35-36, TPT).

The Amplified Bible translates part of verse 35 thus: "...your gentleness and condescension has made me great." His love took up the cross, dying a shameful death. The King of Kings with a twisted crown of thorns placed on His head, our Lord of Lords was robed in scorn and disdained for me and you. Carrying cross and shame, He reclaimed our stolen identity and joy.

What an impactful, life-changing sacrifice He became for us! A healing balm for the trauma and pain that would otherwise scream at our worthlessness 24/7, eight days a week.

From Our *Whys* To God's Wonders

Beauty for Ashes—Glory for Shame

What beauty has come from your ashes?

_____
_____
_____

How has God's glory removed your shame?

_____
_____
_____

> *"If we share our story with someone who responds with empathy and understanding, shame can't survive."* —Brene Brown

Reclaiming Prayer

Thank You, Jesus, for reclaiming all my shame as You stooped down in gentleness to make me great. Your love is so generous, overflowing with complete healing into every area of brokenness, making me whole.

Chapter 9

Forgiveness Takes Courage

The Lord Forgives You And Helps You Forgive

"God, I invite your searching gaze into my heart. Examine me through and through; find out everything that may be hidden within me. Put me to the test and sift through all my anxious cares."
—Psalm 139:23 (TPT)

A Prayer For Courage

One evening, our church had the pleasure of having Chris Overstreet come to share. Chris is an evangelist and the president and founder of Compassion to Action. After his anointed teaching and prophetic words, he asked anyone who wanted courage to come up for prayer. Before I go any further, I need to tell you that on that night, I came into the service heartbroken; I was grieving a relationship that was strained to the core. My mind was plagued with, "What did I do wrong, and how can I make it right?" Hurt mingled and danced with sadness – pain so great I was unaware I was still waltzing to the tune of unforgiveness. Apparently, my dance card was wide open to cut a rug dancing with the devil.

Making my way up to the front for prayer, I was thinking *yes, Lord, I do want the courage to speak up when You ask me to.* Halfheartedly in a melancholy Eeyore fashion, I moped up to the front for prayer, with my tail between my legs. Bowing my head, people surrounded me in prayer, and then it happened.

Someone said, "I feel like you have been hurt by someone." Uncontrollable tears streamed down my face; my mascara was now a spitting image of Alice Cooper. If you youngins don't know who he is, Google him or allow me to translate it for you: me and my mascara were a collective hot mess. Mind racing with thoughts of wanting to run to the bathroom to stop the flow of tears and streaking black mascara, King Solomon's familiar words from Ecclesiastes 1:2 came to mind, " Vanity oh vanity." And so, dismissing the urge, I pushed through the mild-blubbering void of tissue and dignity.

Ears now fully tuned into what was being spoken, I humbly stayed right where God wanted me. I heard the young man say, "It is not you," and as I shared more of the situation, he asked me the million-dollar question, "Have you forgiven them?" My reply was about as tenacious as my mascara. "I'm working on it," I eked out. He asked me if I wanted to forgive, and I, of course, said yes! After the prayer, my heart was lighter, and so were my eyelashes from no more mascara. The tune of unforgiveness ceased; the toehold the enemy had on my dance floor demolished.

Choosing to forgive takes courage, and that fortitude needs to be readily accessible every day with Jesus' help. Taking up offenses and unforgiveness robs us of our joy and cuts off the flow of the fresh life-giving water our loving Father graced us with.

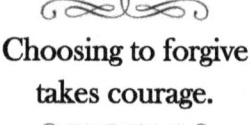

Choosing to forgive takes courage.

Cowardly To Courageous

You may be able to relate to the Cowardly Lion from *The Wizard of OZ*. At one time in his life, he belted out with false bravado and great conviction he was born a sissy. However, you are not and never will be. The label the Cowardly Lion stuck on himself peeled off like a cheap tag. Living purposefully, he saw the real truth that he did indeed have the courage to upstage the bombast facade rooted in a lie. His stick-to-itiveness to pursue healing brought forth untapped gold within Him. You have it too, missy and mister. Now, go roar like you never did before.

Searching Our Hearts

There are times that in order to restore our God-given joy, it might require us to search our hearts. Unforgiveness and bitterness can cause foundational cracks in our faith; joy slips through them. These cracks are produced by seismic waves that have gone undetected, even generational sins, including unforgiveness that have been passed down unto the third and fourth generation. Moses describes this in Exodus 34:7, along with the remedy to correct it: God's unrelenting love for each one of us.

Lord, Your endless love stretches
from one eternity to the other,
unbroken and unrelenting toward those who fear You
and those who bow face down in awe before You.
Your faithfulness to keep every gracious promise You've made
passes from parents to children to grandchildren and beyond.
(Psalm 103:17, TPT, paraphrased)

Generational curses are broken, and sin is forgiven as the door swings wide open to His love and freedom. "Ask, and the gift is yours. Seek, and you'll discover. Knock, and the door will be opened for you. For every persistent one will get what he asks for. Every persistent seeker will discover what he longs for. And everyone who knocks persistently will one day find an open door" (Matthew 7:7-8, TPT).

Lions, Tigers, And Bears

And don't forget unforgiveness, bitterness, and anger...oh my! Add resentment and holding a grudge, and it becomes more reasons to be afraid, very afraid. All these things should be taken seriously when we are searching our hearts before the Lord. If we allow these emotions to remain unchecked, we can slowly but surely develop a hard heart in their presence. God's Word is very clear on all these sins that produce hardheartedness in us. I always like to look up words in the dictionary to shed new light on them.

Let's look at the meaning of some familiar words from the Oxford Language Dictionary, followed by scripture of how to overcome them. As you read the definitions afresh, ask the Holy Spirit to illuminate any words that bring the desire to experience greater depths of healing and wholeness, turning any cold and stony portions of our heart into a heart of flesh.

"And I will give you a new heart, and I will put a new spirit in you. I will take out your stony, stubborn heart and give you a tender, responsive heart" (Ezekiel 36:26, NLT).

A Stony Heart

Definition of Unforgiveness

1. not willing to forgive or excuse people's faults or wrongdoings

2. (of conditions) harsh; hostile

Definition of Bitterness

1. anger and disappointment at being treated unfairly; resentment

Definition of Anger

1. a strong feeling of annoyance, displeasure, or hostility

Definition of Resentment

1. bitter indignation at having been treated unfairly

Definition of Grudge

1. a persistent feeling of ill will or resentment resulting from a past insult or injury

Pause and ask the Lord if any of these applies to you, then read the scriptures below to foster healing in those areas.

Reclaiming Hearts Of Flesh

Unforgiveness Healing Scripture

"But instead be kind and affectionate toward one another. Has God graciously forgiven you? Then graciously forgive one another in the depths of Christ's love..." (Ephesians 4:32, TPT).

Bitterness Healing Scripture

"Lay aside bitter words, temper tantrums, revenge, profanity, and insults" (Ephesians 4:31, TPT).

Anger Healing Scripture

"Stay away from anger and revenge. Keep envy far from you, for it only leads you into lies" (Psalm 37:8, TPT).

Resentment Healing Scripture

"...chasing after things instead of God, manipulating others, hatred of those who get in your way, senseless arguments, resentment when others are favored, temper tantrums, angry quarrels, only thinking of yourself, being in love with your own opinions ..." (Galatians 5:20, TPT).

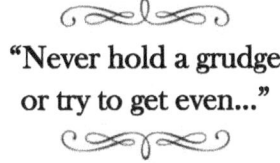

"Never hold a grudge or try to get even..."

Grudge Healing Scripture

"Never hold a grudge or try to get even, but plan your life around the noblest way to benefit others. Do your best to live as everybody's friend. Beloved, don't be obsessed with taking revenge, but leave that to God's righteous justice. For the Scriptures say: 'Vengeance is mine, and I will repay,' says the Lord" (Romans 12:17-19, TPT).

Welcome the Holy Spirit in all areas of your life, bringing refreshment to your heart and mind. Doing that one move toward healing will never disappoint and will untangle all the knotted-up lies that hinder your spiritual fluidity.

Untangled

When my husband and I were just friends, he walked to my house occasionally to hang out before he had a car. On his journey one day, he found a sturdy blue Goody comb. Happily, he picked it up to take it home later and boil it. I'm pretty sure he would not do that nowadays. Pulling it out of his pocket like Indiana Jones, he held it up with glee to show me his rich treasure. He was so excited about his comb. Believe me, I tried to have the same level of enthusiasm he possessed with his newfound gem. I fear it might have been faint *yay*...arms half raised to add a little oomph. Sadly, nowhere near the beam of Kevin's smile.

However, I did treasure Kevin's heart and the joy he found in the simple things, which is one of the many things I love about him. Almost 35 years later, we still have this treasured comb nestled safely in a basket in our bathroom. From time to time, we joked about framing it. Through the years, occasionally, Kevin had false alarms that he had lost it. Yet it was always joyfully found.

We, too, can get just as excited as Kevin was about his comb if we let the Lord use His beloved fine-toothed, spiritual Goody comb to work through any tangled sin areas, unraveling the twisted emotion, releasing it to glide smoothly, unobstructed. When I was young, having my mom comb through my long hair to untangle it was never a fun process. Finally, Johnson's came out with a product called No More Tears, No More Tangles, letting the comb guide through with far fewer snags. However, either way, my mom and I both knew the work had to be done to prevent a bigger and far more painful problem if left untouched.

And by the way, Jesus is by far the best detangler ever. No more tears, no more tangles...oh goody!

Bitterness To Bobby Pins

The first retreat Tetelestai Ministries held was at Camp Crestview Retreat in February 2020. I attended alone, moving away from carpools and the usual comforts and security of palling around with my friends. Though there is nothing wrong with hanging around with friends, it was just a gentle nudge from Jesus to go solo. It did not take long to be surrounded by some new and some familiar faces; that was comforting in a whole new way. Out of my comfort zone was indeed a lovely place to be.

The first night, I saw my bubbly, precious friend Peggy. If you have the pleasure of knowing her, you know she is 100 % pure joy! Bouncing up to me, all smiles and laughter, she provided a warm hug to seal the deal of feeling loved. Peggy is good at that.

It was not long after when she began to reminisce of how delightful, prophetic, and funny my mom had been. Continuing with a humorous story of the three of us guffawing it up in a department store years ago, we laughed as heartily that night as we did years ago, only this time without my mom. Heading to my chair, I realized the warm fuzzies that were spoken of my mom left me feeling a tad flatline, which had me thinking. I grabbed my pen, positioned my heart, and jotting in my journal. I asked the Lord this question: "Do I harbor bitterness toward my mom?"

Though I felt I had done all the necessary work in our relationship before and after her passing, it was beginning to dawn on me a root of unforgiveness and bitterness was still lodged in my heart, buried deep. I knew that night it had to come out.

Because God is so faithful to reveal what He wants to heal, that night, He literally brought me to the four wooden crosses on stage to become free. Each cross erected was painted with red paint to signify Jesus' blood shed for you and me. Standing before the cross, we were encouraged to grab ahold of the magnitude of Jesus' forgiveness as we released anything that needed to stay on the cross once and for all.

Laying my hands on the fresh red paint, I cried and asked for forgiveness of any bitterness and unforgiveness still in my heart toward my mama. As I stood at the crosses, waiting for answers, a picture was revealed to me: I saw a lock of brown hair just like my mom's being released from a bobby pin, which is what she always used to pin-curl her hair for as long as I could remember. It was a sign of release. It would not be the last time the Lord would speak to me with those little gems, for they took me from bitterness to bobby pins to blessings.

Bobby Pins To Blessings

In the summer of 2020, I had the pleasure of attending another weekend event at Camp Crestview. This time, I was accompanied by my two dear friends Lynn A. and Debbie. The teaching and worship were amazing as we sat in the amphitheater overlooking the Columbia River, which is nothing short of breathtaking. As the day wore on, the sun rays beat down on us, causing my friends to long for shade, which was a divine setup. As they moved away, someone sat next to me, listening to the wonderful teaching.

Suddenly, I had overwhelming thoughts of unforgiveness toward someone (not my two friends). I frantically grabbed my Bible and started flipping like a mad woman to get relief, for it was intense and tormenting. Not long after the person stopped in the middle of her teaching, I thought I was busted for acting like a mad woman. Prompted by the Holy Spirit, she called for those needing prayer, and boy did I.

The woman next to me and Pastor Jeremy prayed for me, and it was pure heaven. Tears streamed down my face. Does this sound familiar? And, yes, you got it. Once again, mascara streaming down right along with them. Right there, I finally got the memo: from now on, only wear waterproof mascara.

Turning to the woman next to me to thank her for her prayers, I asked, "Do I have mascara on my face?" She sweetly said, "Yes, a little there, and there, and little there," etc. She then said, "But wasn't it worth it?" I wholeheartedly agreed, but still excused myself to clean up my face; my heart was free and joyful.

Once in the bathroom, I took my phone out of my pocket to place on the bench, and to my great surprise, three bobby pins were lined next to each other on the bench. Overjoyed, I put the bobby pins in my shorts pocket, and later that afternoon, I got baptized, with the pins still in my pocket. Don't you just love how God shows His love to us?

Forgive And Forgive Some More

When it comes to the hard things, I'm a fan of the *one and done*. Unfortunately, if you have lived very long, you know life can be hard, and *one and done* are few and far between. And yet, there is this truth: sweetness comes in hard places, promises of honey from the rock of our circumstances. Side by side, Jesus is there to help us endure things, to overcome things that test us. He wants to see us grow; He wants to bring forth gold and, of course, honey in all of us, which is always comforting.

> **Sweetness can be found in hard places.**

Still, with all the promise of goodness coming forth in hard places, I have a hunch that when Peter asked Jesus about forgiveness in Matthew 18:21-31, it probably was not the answer he had hoped for. It seemed like he was a one-and-done person just like me. As he approached Jesus that day, he, too, asked a million-dollar question.

"How many times do I have to forgive my fellow believer who keeps offending me? Seven times?"

Jesus answered, "Not seven times, Peter, but seventy times seven times!"

In Hebrew, the number seven is a word for completeness or wholeness. Perhaps Peter chose the number to feel if he forgave someone seven times a day, he could check it off his list of to-dos.

That, too, sounds like me.

But Jesus' parable after His answer to Peter makes you ponder the magnitude of God's forgiveness in an epic way. In this story, a king chose to show mercy, forgiving the begging servant of his massive, one-billion-dollar debt, only to find out that the forgiven servant showed no mercy to another. Choking him in anger, this same servant refused to forgive a fellow servant a mere 20-thousand-dollar debt. Infuriated, the king brought severe punishment to the unmerciful servant, turning him over to the prison guards to be tortured until all his debts were repaid.

We have been forgiven much; let's pay it forward.

It makes you think long and hard about how we need to forgive others just as Christ has forgiven us. We have been forgiven much; let's pay it forward...70x7.

At The Cross Again

My dad accepted the Lord as His Savior as his last days on earth were drawing to a close, losing his battle with cancer at age 53. In fact, before this answer to prayer for his salvation, the Lord had told me he would have to be on his back before he would ever look up to Him. And that is exactly what happened; his laryngeal cancer metastasized to his bones, leaving him flat on his back until the day he died, and by God's grace, he was carried to heaven.

I was 27 years old when my dad was dying and still had no idea about his abuse toward me. During the six-month lifespan they gave my dad, I worked on healing our relationship as best I could with what I knew at the time. As I shared earlier, it was 20 years later, at 47 years old, that the confirmation came to begin to uncover the abuse by my father. At the time, I thought I had fully forgiven him, walking those many miles on that well-worn path to get there. When we press into Jesus, we get the joy of becoming freer each passing day, and though I'm in my 60s, I love each day we can walk in more freedom. I say, sign me up.

One day, a while back, I asked the Lord to show me any area that He wants to work on in my life. Though I was aware of some things, I did not realize I had been apathetic with my thoughts toward my dad just as I had with my mom until I watched the TBN Good Friday Worldwide special during the COVID-19 pandemic. As I got comfortable on the sofa, I tuned in right when Chris Tomlin was singing "At the Cross" with a large cross in the background. When I looked at him singing, he looked like my dad as a young man. In all the times I have seen Chris Tomlin, that was the first time he reminded me of my dad.

I wept at the sight of that beautiful smile and the shape of his face. Compassion flooded my heart in a whole new way for my dad. A fresh release of joy and peace filled my heart and mind that evening, all because I asked the Lord to truly search my heart. I want to walk in it all the days of my life, and I know you do too.

The truth is, Chris Tomlin sang with such joy; a joy my dad was not able to grab ahold of until his dying days. And now, he smiles with a love and freedom he could never have experienced here on earth. As I sat in awe of seeing my dad in a whole new light, with tears still flowing, Chris asked us to sing "Amazing Grace." I knew my chains were gone, and I had been set free. What a perfect song to sing at that moment, because my chains were gone just like my dad's. And to all those people who said I looked like him when I was growing up, right now, I sure hope I do.

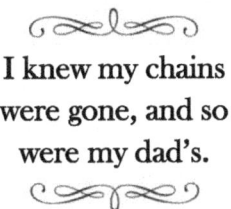

I knew my chains were gone, and so were my dad's.

Double-Dipping Into Psalms 139

In Chapter 1, we had the privilege to ponder all of Psalms 139, and as you know, each chapter starts with a selected verse from that very same chapter. It seems like I cannot get enough of chapter 139. I had to go in for another serving.

Pondering this Psalm again with my second scoop, I realize this chapter has a sweet and salty flavor to it. David starts with honeyed words, dripping sweetness of God's extravagant intimacy, understanding Him in His totality. He is full of gratitude, aware that every movement, shortcoming, and word that comes out of his mouth never surprises God. I'm so thankful for that truth. When a word as salty as a sailor's has flown out of my mouth in anger, in private moments when a hammer hits an emotional trigger hidden to me (yet not to God), I'm comforted. Though it catches me off guard, it never once did Him.

Verses 1 to 18 go on a steady, slow drip of honey from the silver spoon. Well-deserved praise rolls off his tongue to the Pure and Shining One. When, all of a sudden, the brakes were slammed on, King David backed into reverse as quickly as he had once moved forward. Honey no longer drips; instead, salt pours out as our taste buds detect that a tang has now entered the mix.

David's anger rises as he recounts the sins of the wicked and blood-thirsty men who he was all too familiar with. He certainly had his share of run-ins with them. The juxtaposition of this familiar chapter has not changed since my last read; it just became highlighted and underlined. It reveals the incredible intrinsic value of our birth and all of God's woven tapestry of intricacies in stark contrast to our adversaries and our own sinfulness.

Perhaps it did not take David long to realize that when we back up the trolley, we not only see the things that lay behind us if our rear-view mirror is tilted just right, but it also holds our own reflection. Humbled, he soon realized he, too, had sinned and fallen short of the glory of God, as I, too, have recognized in myself far too many times to count. As the saying goes, if you point a finger at someone, all the rest point back at you.

David knew the importance of inviting His loving Heavenly Father to search his heart to examine him through and through. He invited God to find anything and everything that may be hidden and causing him to walk a path of pain, giving Him full permission to guide him back to God's glorious ways.

Our desperate need to know our value, worth and identity is deeply rooted in the knowledge of His elaborate love for each one of us. For those of us who have faced trauma inside or outside of the womb (or both), our image of God can be severely tainted. The natural progression of Psalms 139 is a beautiful template for our own lives to see our worth and to see our need.

From Our *Whys* To God's Wonders

1. On a separate piece of paper, write down anyone who comes to mind that you have been hurt by. Then, ask the Lord to help you forgive and ask for forgiveness in areas where you have held any unforgiveness, bitterness, or anger toward them. Burn or tear up the page; you can even write 'forgiven' in red before you do it.

2. Pick one or two people you might be struggling with in the forgiveness department. Write or speak all the great qualities they possess. It helps to defuse any bitterness that wants to take root.

3. Where do you feel the Lord's forgiveness in your life?

_____
_____
_____

4. How has that forgiveness changed you?

_____
_____
_____

Reclaiming Prayer

Heavenly Father, we thank You for Your forgiveness toward us. We want to walk in that same posture of forgiving freely as You have forgiven us. Correct any area in my life where bitterness or unforgiveness has taken root and bring me to Your cross with a repentant heart (turning toward You and away from what saddens You). Allow bitter waters to now flow sweet. Today, I choose to partner to become better, not bitter, and walk in my newfound freedom, declaring Your goodness every step of the way.

I will walk in greater levels of healing and forgiveness each passing day as I seek You, Lord.

Chapter 10

Closed Door, Opened Window

The Lord Makes a Way

"See if there is any path of pain I'm walking on, and lead me back to your glorious, everlasting way—the path that brings me back to you."
—Psalm 139:24 (TPT)

Room With A View

As I write this, I'm sitting in my redecorated bedroom with a view. The view I speak of does not carry breathtaking snow-covered mountain peaks or dramatic, crashing waves against the shoreline. It's a rather plain view looking out to our fence and small side yard. In the last 27 years, we have seen changes not only in this yard but the room I now occupy. Once, this room held two little precious boys I would tuck into bed with a kiss and a prayer. Boys sweet with their occasional rough and tumble ways, sharing giggles, imaginations, not to mention their frustrations, hopes, and dreams. And from time to time, growing up, they would shoot infamous amounts of 6mm Airsoft BBs from the window ledge. Those precious boys became incredible men who we could not be more proud of or love any more.

God's Filter

Our lives are full of changes and seasons. Some, we celebrate, and some, not so much. And with those changes and seasons, our views and perspectives can change for better or worse. If our faith in God is built on the knowledge of His goodness, the lens we peer through will transform our outlook, shifting our understanding into a Kingdom perspective. Hardships, disappointment, and loss come into focus, redecorated by His love that filters out our human reasoning. Now His bigger picture shines with fresh revelations of our *whys*. Being able to see beyond a shadow of a doubt, his words of wonder are meant for good and not evil, to give us a future and a hope that will not disappoint us. That is by far the best filter to view through.

"'For I know the plans I have for you,' declares the Lord, 'plans to prosper you and not to harm you, plans to give you hope and a future'" (Jeremiah 29:11, NIV).

All Things And All Seasons

Jeremiah 29:11 is by far one of my favorite life verses. However, it's so hard to choose because God's Word is so yummy. I do, however, love to quote Philippians 4:13 a lot, which declares, "I have strength for all things in Christ Who empowers me [I am ready for anything and equal to anything through Him Who infuses inner strength into me; I am self-sufficient in Christ's sufficiency]" (AMPC). This especially applies when I need brute physical strength to drag a piece of heavy furniture across the room when my hubby is not home. Or for my need for emotional strength when the weight of this life has spiritually made me feel puny.

Flexing our spiritual muscles is a Holy Spirit burn we need to feel to keep us strong in His truths. Recently, we heard a pastor explain Philippians 4:13 in a way I'd never heard before. He put it this way: "I can do all seasons through Christ who strengthens me." That really resonated with me. We need God's strength in all our seasons. I needed it as a child, a teenager, a young woman newly divorced, when battling an eating disorder and shattered dreams. I needed it when I became a blushing bride full of renewed hope. Now, as I reach my golden years, using my time wisely for God's promises, my latter years will be better than my former.

I don't know where your life has taken you – your hopes, the big dreams you have dreamed, or the crushing heartache you have encountered in your life so far. However, this I do know: you can always count on Jesus Christ to be faithful in every season and all things. You will always find His strength to guide you as you co-labor through every promise and struggle filled with synergy, for you never walk alone.

Whys To His Wonder

Sitting in this room with a view, so much has changed in the 27 years we have lived here. It's the same window we thought we would have replaced by now, but besides that, this room's decor has changed through the seasons as the boys grew up and their tastes changed. And once our oldest moved out, this room eventually became a place of deeper healing for me. With that in mind in this chapter, I would like to share with you how this room helped change my view about God and how through it all I hope you see more of how the God of wonders can work so beautifully even in our *whys*.

Dream Home

I can still remember the day we toured this house; it was truly like a dream. Kevin and I had lived in an apartment for eight years, and now with two boys ages three and one respectively, my heart cry was for them to have a backyard to play in. It was the subject of many of my prayers, and after what felt like years, we finally were able to get a loan and started our house hunting.

The day the realtor had an appointment for us to see a house, Kevin said, "I'm running late; tell her to give us an address closer to the city we want." The housing market at that time was far more pricey and less bang for your buck; our realtor was trying to get us more home for our money. To be perfectly honest, I was mad at my husband, thinking he was dragging his feet on the house hunt. I, like so many times in my life, was chomping at

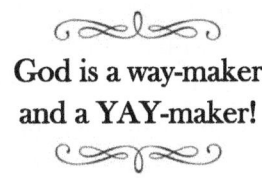

God is a way-maker and a YAY-maker!

the bit. It just goes to show you how wrong I can be, for God's delays are never His denials. What we don't see in the natural, He is preparing a way when there seems to be no way. He's not only a way maker, but He is also a yay maker.

We piled in the car, and I gave my husband the address. Still fuming, I didn't even realize he was taking us to the neighborhood I loved so dearly. It was the neighborhood where he lived with a friend, and I would drop them off after church. At the time, I was recently divorced and a full-blown anorexic; I felt like I really didn't fit in anywhere anymore.

Driving down Ash Street after church to drop them off, I was utterly broken with not much hope or belief that I would ever marry again, let alone have kids. Little did I know what was in store. Not only would I marry Kevin, but I would also live in the cute little neighborhood I always loved, have two boys, and would one day live a block away from Ash Street – one block away from the street where I thought my life was over. God truly gives us beauty for ashes and the oil of joy for mourning. Never underestimate what God can do with ashes, even if you were the cause of the blaze.

Grief Knocks At The Door

Our boys shared this room until they were teenagers. Our son Derek got a job with a swing shift, turning our family room into our bedroom, making it more conducive for the boys. Before Derek moved out, my once very independent mother had moved in with us. This life-changing occurrence happened suddenly. One day, she did not answer her phone, which was highly unusual of her. I had a strong sense deep inside me something was wrong. My husband and I rushed to her nearby apartment, pounding on the door. In our rush, I had forgotten my keys to her apartment. My heart pounded too as each knock and call out brought no response. Quickly, I ran to the apartment manager's office for Mom's apartment key. As I almost got to the office door, I heard Kevin yell, "She's alive."

Overjoyed, I ran back, only to find her incoherent, half-dressed, somehow still able to crawl to the door to answer it. Kneeling, I hugged her; I was just so happy she was alive, yet I knew in my heart her life might never be the same. Strange thing is, ten years prior to this I had a dream very similar to this same scenario, just in a different apartment. Doctors said she had blown a heart valve, and because of her dementia, they would not operate on her. We already had a growing concern about her declining mental health; however, the doctor's diagnosis validated them. Now, with that knowledge and a doctor's backing, it made it a bit easier to get this strong, independent woman the help she would have most likely refused before.

Sadly, as this was going on, my brother had already been diagnosed with Lewy Body dementia. Having them both suffer from dementia at the same time only compounded my sense of loss. I braced myself for the inevitability of losing both of them; it was only a matter of time. Wanting to spend time with them, yet we'd walk away from our visits emotionally and physically wiped as a result of grief and overwhelming sadness.

I said goodbye to normal things at that moment, because my new normal was having to buckle up my independent mom and strap my brother into their car seats, which was beyond heartbreaking. An extreme sense of loneliness that I had never known before swept across my soul, not to mention all the loss of memory, communication, and everyday activities we can so easily take for granted. I thank God they both remembered me until their dying days. With God's help I tried my best to live in my new reality, savoring every memory I could, even in the pain of it all.

I was well on my way to becoming the sole survivor of the family I once grew up in. It was not a place I thought I would be in at my age; the feelings of survivor's guilt had rolled around in my head as to why this happened. At times, I would ask the Lord if He thought the convergence of aging parents, menopause, and adult children moving out was a really good idea. It seemed a bit much. I was comforted by what the prophet Isaiah penned in Isaiah 55:8-9 (AMPC): "'For My thoughts are not your thoughts, neither are your ways My ways,' says the Lord. 'For as the heavens are higher than the earth, so are My ways higher than your ways and My thoughts than your thoughts.'"

Bird's Eye View

Looking back at it all from a bird's eye view, I see God's hand more clearly, and the mere jagged rubble of the heart-wrenching *whys* removed to open a place of surrender to His loving sovereignty.

Something else happened in this season of overwhelming day-to-day grief. My intentions were at times misread or misunderstood in regards to the handling of my mom and brother, which made the season all the more painful. Looking back, I could have handled some things differently. Grief can knock the stuffing out of us as we process our loss. Be mindful that others, too, are walking through their own grief, coping to the best of their ability as they handle the imminent loss looming over everyone involved.

Grace is essential to navigating grief, which poses to be complex, dicey, and unique to each person's personality. Grace to ourselves and others is the hinge pin to swinging the door open to the other (victorious) side of grief. The Kubler-Ross model points out the five stages of grief as follows: denial, anger, depression, bargaining, and acceptance. Still, each of these stages might not be processed in the same way. Grief is messy, comes in waves, and there is no cookie-cutter-mold way of handling it.

This not only pertains to grief, but, in general, circumstances that can appear totally different than they actually are, building a false case against someone. Grief only magnifies misconceptions. Ask the person their intentions if in doubt, and try to give them the benefit when it warrants it. The bottom line is, God knows our hearts. If there is any

What the enemy means for evil, God will use it for good.

wrongdoing, God will make it right. If you have been misunderstood, our integrity will shine through; it might just not happen overnight. It gets darkest before dawn, and out of that darkness, God wastes not one drop of our pain. What the enemy means for evil, we know God will use it for good.

In high school, my photography class had a darkroom to develop our camera film from photos we took for class projects. Once the photo paper was placed in the developer solution, we'd agitate it by rocking the tray back and forth until the picture came to life. There are times in our life when our situations look dark and rather hopeless. However, someday, God will reveal the bigger picture, and you will emerge from the darkness with a clear picture that God was with you the whole time. His filter of love and understanding is picture-perfect, turning our negatives into positives.

I Go And Prepare A Place For You

Unfortunately, my mom had to be moved into assisted living only after a couple of months of living with us due to her repeatedly falling in our bathroom. Our tiny bathroom could not properly fit her needs, and our attempt to make sure she had assistance was lost due to her dementia. Not only was it sad to have her go, finding someone who would take care of her with love and dignity was like looking for a needle in a haystack. Not because there are no caring facilities out there; we just did not have the funds to pay her rent and Medicaid was not the payment of choice for a good portion of adult care facilities. So, we were faced with multiple dilemmas: lack of funds, a possible waiting list, a place we felt safe to have her live, and of course, somewhere she wanted to live seemed next to nil.

The Lord did open up a temporary respite care at an adult care center. We not only had peace of mind, knowing she no longer would fall in our bathroom, but He also gave me more time to look for a permanent place for her to live without having to move her again.

One day, while visiting her, I was so sad and weary of searching for the perfect place to entrust her to. After we chatted a bit, I turned the T.V. to her favorite Christian station right when a pastor was teaching from John chapter 14. This was the very same chapter I had turned to by accident the day my mom got the call from the doctor that her puffy ankles could be related to her heart only a few months earlier.

And right then and there, I was hearing this promise again...

"Do not let your hearts be troubled (distressed, agitated). You believe in and adhere to and trust in and rely on God; believe in and adhere to and trust in and rely also on Me. In my Father's house there are many dwelling places (homes). If it were not so, I would have told you; for I am going away to prepare a place for you. And when I go and make ready a place for you, I will come back again and will take you to Myself, that where I am you may be also. And to the place where I am going you know the way" (John 14:1-4, AMPC).

Standing behind my mom, rubbing her shoulders, I prayed, "God, please prepare a way where there seems to be no way." He also brought to mind Jeremiah 33:3 (AMPC): "Call to Me and I will answer you and show you great and mighty things, fenced in and hidden, which you do not know (do not distinguish and recognize, have knowledge of and understanding."

The Miracle Number

It was not long after that when the Lord opened a door to a lovely home with a small number of folks – a place where Mom felt more at home. It was nestled back off the road with a long side fence (fenced in and hidden just like my promise verse), with an adult foster home that belonged to Mom's caregiver's parents in the front. This gave me an extra measure of comfort for Mom's safety if she somehow, God forbid, got out and wandered off. My mom loved her caregiver and her two-year-old son. She was also beyond accommodating with our coverage, encouraging me when I was in utter tears over the financial piece that had been such a roadblock.

Finally, I began to feel peace about her living there as much as one can in that situation, yet the Lord knew I needed an extra hug to my heart in this difficult decision. So, He added the cherry on top by having the address of her new, beautiful home be 717. Yes, that's right; Brent's and my birthday. He did prepare a place for Mom on earth as He did in heaven.

One day, when my mom was under her care, I picked up a cute little mug at the thrift store. The mug's front had a picture of a vintage phone in black and white, with a saying underneath that read "Jesus is my wake-up call." Not long after that, unbeknownst to Mom's care provider, the name *Jesus* started showing up from time to time on caller ID when she called me. Hey, when I see Jesus calling, I'm going to answer it!

Jesus' name would pop up from time to time and became a beautiful comfort in the early morning of Mom's passing on May 1st of 2013. Jesus was truly my wake-up call, for Mom's caregiver's phone ID said so. What a signpost of comfort from God. When I asked her about it after Mom's passing, she did not even know it was showing up as her ID. I love how God is always wanting to talk to us. We just simply need to look and listen for it.

Sadly, my brother passed away three short years later on March 17th, 2016. Even so, the Lord is always faithful in all the seasons of our lives. We can trust Him with all our *whys* and sorrows.

Room To Change

This room I now sit in, with its changing view, had become a memorial to my mother, brother, and our family's past and present after Derek moved out. It stayed as such for nearly seven years, functioning mainly as a place to display memories and store things. At times, God will slowly change our view, excavating it from darkness into a brighter horizon, seeing our circumstances from a higher and more glorious perspective.

"We throw open our doors to God and discover at the same time He has already thrown open His doors to us. We find ourselves standing where we always hoped we might stand out in the wide-open spaces of God's grace and glory standing tall and shouting our praise" (Romans 5:1-2, MSG).

One night in November of 2019, I had a dream of additional rooms in our existing home. One room had the number 15 and the old-fashioned L. C. Smith typewriter my sweet friend Lisa bought me. Recalling my dream, I remember saying in it that I would now have more room. When I awoke, I thought it was odd, even though through the first eight years of living in our 700 ft. home, I had many dreams of a bigger home with growing boys and a shrinking house. That was when tiny homes were not the cat's meow, for back then, it seemed the bigger the home, the better.

In the eight years of occasionally dreaming in my wake and sleep times, my dream became a reality following the addition of a 538 ft. great room and kitchen. Our new kitchen was a nice size, no longer described as a one-butt only kitchen (or one *derriere*...a tad more classy, I suppose). Gone also was the fear of having Popeye the Sailor Man's arms from lifting the microwave off the counter to do dishes by hand every day. So, that new dream with new rooms was hung out to dry, waiting along with all the other times I was unsure of a word or dream needing the Lord's revelation. Much to my surprise and excitement, the revealing of my dream came only one month later in early December.

No More Gloom

I was preparing for a Women's Conference titled Lavish; it was part of Her Voice put on by the Tetelestai Ministers. They suggested beforehand that the women would fast from something of our choosing to put us on the fast track, removing distractions. Fasting allows one's heart to hear God more clearly, opening doors to receive deeper levels of healing. I accepted the challenge and removed something in my life that had been an albatross around my neck for years.

The conference was life-changing, not just because of the amazing worship, wonderful teaching, or the thoughtful gifts meant to represent the lavish love of God. It was an atmosphere of praise, expectancy, and a deep heart cry for intimacy with our Creator. He was welcomed, and His healing power flowed throughout the entire weekend gathering, setting women free all around the room. This freedom is available to all who seek His face wherever and whenever. As mentioned before, He is no respecter of persons.

On the first night of the conference, it was a 'Whiteout night' with prior encouragement to wear a white top if possible. Stepping onto the elevator from the 15th floor (the number 15 from my dream; more to come about that later in the chapter), all the white outfits made it seem like the elevator was full of angels. What a beautiful sight it was. But I felt a strong urge to tell anyone boarding that no, they hadn't died and they weren't getting into an angelic elevator on their way up to heaven.

Upon arriving, it was already 7 pm, time for the meeting. We stepped into a beautiful, all-white room, with white butterfly fur chairs circling the stage; white sections of fur rugs snugged tightly together blanketed the floors seamlessly.

Days before the conference, God was already beginning to stir something deep inside me. Little touches of His grace were gently becoming known to me. On one particular day, a loving nudge from Him drew my attention to see Scooby's dog collar hanging on the rearview mirror. I had placed it there a couple of years ago after he had passed away. Suddenly, I realized I didn't want it up there anymore. Slowly, I removed it to keep it in a memory box. It was a light airy feeling of freedom and forward movement. My time of holding on and looking back through a dark, heavy cloud of grief was slowly being lifted. I had no idea this would be the beginning of a journey that would ultimately end my prolonged spirit of mourning.

Returning home from the conference, I was brimming full of joy and a renewed sense of hope, and in tow, carrying my white fur butterfly chair along with two sections of white rugs they had graciously given us. Now came the dilemma: where can I put these new treasures so our dog Buddy won't destroy them? He'd already pooped on my zebra print rug, and it had to be thrown away. Mind you, that pretty much was the only rug in our house. Really, Buddy?! This rug was the focal point of our black and white room with aqua walls. A shrine, a storage room, and a place where a dog can poop, apparently.

The zebra rug's demise was a mere prelude to the coming attraction of what God had in mind to transform that *room of mourning* into a *room of JOY*. It was now going to be my new little sanctuary to soak in God's love. The black curtains came down, as well as the black lamps, black chair, and dark pillows, yet still joyfully displaying my beloved L. C. Smith Typewriter, a nod for my call to write.

The room with a new view was updated with my white chair, white rugs, renewed inspiration, and a closed-door policy for Buddy! The darkness of grief that had lingered under the radar far too long had now outworn its welcome and had been replaced with light. This fresh perspective ushered out the mourning. That little haven of fresh hope, life, and light now streams through its reclaimed space. It served its purpose for years; it honored my mom and brother and still does...just differently. Honestly, I know that is what they would want for me. The cleverly disguised gloom (room) that entrenched my soul was lifted; the grieving process has had adequate time to heal.

Spent Time With Him

Sitting here today, writing this book on my computer (not my L. C. Smith Typewriter), I am amazed how a room that lay fallow for seven years is back to life. Jeremiah 4:3 (AMPC) talks about this. "Break up your ground left uncultivated for a season, so that you may not sow among thorns."

This room is no longer a step in and out to stow and go, but my haven to journal, worship and pray. It is brimming with time well spent at Jesus' feet while I allow God to repair the ruins of my life to joyful wonder and restoration.

You do not need a physical room designated for journaling, prayer, or having your quiet time. Though it's nice to have a place to meet God, a place of solitude, space does not always permit that.

I remember hearing the story of John and Charles Wesley; these two spiritual giants had a praying mama who covered her head with her apron for her designated two-hour quiet time while her ten children read, studied, or played around her. This became an effective way for her children to know she was having her special time with the Lord. One of my friends lit a candle to signal a quiet, uninterrupted time. However you choose time to carve away for Jesus, you will never regret it.

"You will show me the path of life; in Your presence is fullness of joy, at Your right hand there are pleasures forevermore" (Psalm 16:11, AMPC). That presence can be acquired when we posture our spirit in prayer, worship, or tuning our ears to listen to Him speak to us. He speaks to us day and night without needing any special room with a view. The only view needed is His Heavenly perspective, and the only room necessary is in our hearts – for welcoming His presence. That, by far, is the best room with a view.

> "You know, the truth that Christ wants my fellowship, that he loves me, wants me to be with him and waits for me, has done more to transform my quiet time with God than any other single fact."
> —Robert Boyd Munger

Journaling has changed my view about God, myself, and life in general. Though I have regular journals, I also started buying the sturdy bound 9x12 sketchbooks as journals as well to draw, paste, and dream. Being a visual learner helps me see images, not just words. Below are some things I have learned about this exciting new way to journal.

Journaling With Jesus

Did you know that journaling can help us with mindfulness and remaining present with our thoughts? The act of journaling gives us an opportunity to express our emotions, when we otherwise may not want to. It can also provide new revelations and greater self-awareness.

A few things I have learned through spending time journaling with Jesus:

First of all, anyone can do this, so do not be intimidated. As you yield to this process, you will find:

He brings deep healing when we draw near to Him and listen to His loving thoughts toward us.

He is delighted that you want to hear His heart toward you and others. He wants to dream big with you!

God is love, and He speaks His love toward us in many ways. Pray for spiritual eyes and ears to see God and His Word in fresh ways.

Be open to new ways to express yourself on the pages of your journal.

Step out and learn to embrace imperfection! It's about opening up and letting go, creating in the style God gave you to create without comparing or feeling inadequate. It's all about you and Father, Son, and Holy Spirit having fun. No one ever has to see it if you don't want them to. Breathe in the breath of God's creativity and go for it! Be free in your personal, judgement-free zone.

Here are a few more ideas for your journal:

Pick an image for your journal's cover. What speaks to you? Maybe it's a picture of what God is doing in your life. My first was a vintage drawing of a baby, because God was bringing me back to healing in the womb and beyond. It does not have to be the theme throughout your whole book. Let it be organic and free-flowing with the Holy Spirit in what He is saying to you. Have fun and be childlike. There is no right or wrong way with your personal journal; that is part of your journey. Think outside of the box and color outside of the lines like no one is watching.

I enjoy using designed craft paper, photos, stickers, or other forms of expression. Using colored pencils, colored pens, sharpie pens, markers, oil pastels, and fine pens to write is always fun. Dollar stores have a good assortment of craft items at cheap prices. I have even bought greeting cards for myself – even a card for a daughter from my Papa Daddy.

Remember to be mindful of what design is speaking to you to ponder with the Lord.

I like to keep the items in one location, which is a good spot to work. The easier you make it, the more you will be apt to do it. You can put it all in a basket to grab if you cannot keep your items in your work location.

If something you are working on is keeping you stuck and you no longer feel inspired, switch gears. You can always go back to the thing you left behind. Remember, we are kicking condemnation, comparison, perfection, and performance to the curb, and we say *good riddance*.

Listening to worship music is a lovely way to soak in His presence while you journal.

Google can be a great tool to find the meaning of things the Lord is saying to you. Of course, His Word is ultimately the best plumbline for truth. He might give me a word I don't know the meaning of or a picture of an item I want to know more about. Write it down or print it out. You might not remember what He told you, but adding a date may help you recall it. Also note that sometimes, you might find yourself on a New Age site. If so, just back up the trolley and move more into a biblical spiritual search. Be discerning with what you are reading.

Finally, dream big. Be full of hope, do what you were created for, ponder the deep thing of God, and listen to His still, small voice, for He is always speaking to you. Always enjoy the delightful treasure hunt of God's goodness that is waiting to be uncovered. Happy digging.

Journaling Has Health Benefits

What are some of the short- and long-term health benefits of putting pen to paper? Here are five, good-for-you virtues of journaling I found at intermountainhealthcare.org/blogs/topics/live-well/2018:

1. It reduces stress: An overabundance of stress can be damaging to your physical, mental, and emotional health. It's proven. Journaling is an incredible stress management tool, a good-for-you habit that lessens the impact of physical stressors on your health. In fact, a study showed that expressive writing (like journaling) for only 15 to 20 minutes a day, three to five times, over a four-month period was enough to lower blood pressure and improve liver functionality. Plus, writing about stressful experiences can help you manage them in a healthy way. Try establishing journaling as a pre-bedtime meditation habit to help you unwind and de-stress.

2. It improves immune function: Believe it or not, expressive writing can strengthen your immunity and decrease your risk of illness. Those who journal boast of improved immune system functioning (it strengthens immune cells), as well as lessened symptoms of asthma and rheumatoid arthritis. Expressive writing has been shown to improve liver and lung functions and combat certain diseases. It has even been reported to help the wounded heal faster.

3. It keeps memory sharp: Journaling helps keep your brain in tip-top shape. Not only does it boost memory and comprehension, but it also increases working memory capacity, which may reflect improved cognitive processing.

4. It boosts mood: Want more sunshine in your life? Try journaling. A unique social and behavioral outcome of journaling is this: it can improve your mood and give you a greater sense of overall emotional well-being and happiness.

5. It strengthens emotional functions: Related to mood is how journaling benefits overall emotional health. As journaling habits are developed, benefits become long-term, meaning that diarists become more in tune with their health by connecting with inner needs and desires. Journaling evokes mindfulness and helps writers remain present while keeping perspective. It presents an opportunity for emotional catharsis and helps the brain regulate emotions. It provides a greater sense of confidence and self-identity. Journaling can help in the management of personal adversity and change and emphasize important patterns and growth in life. Research even shows that expressive writing can help individuals develop more structured, adaptive, and integrated schemes about themselves, others, and the world. What's more, journaling unlocks and engages right-brained creativity, which gives you access to your full brainpower. Truly, journaling fosters growth.

Wait For It

That dream of the extra room with my typewriter and the number 15 hotel room came true. I was a winner, winner, chicken dinner. Let's look again at Habakkuk 2:3–5, this time in The Message Bible: "And then God answered: 'Write this. Write what you see. Write it out in big block letters so that it can be read on the run. This vision-message is a witness pointing to what's coming. It aches for the coming—it can hardly wait! pointing to what's coming. And it doesn't lie. If it seems slow in coming, wait. It's on its way. It will come right on time.'"

"His Word is truth, and He is alert and active, watching over His Word to perform it" (Jeremiah 1:12, AMPC). God is good on His promise to us. You might be walking in deep, agonizing grief of the loss of a loved one, death to a marriage, loss of job, or a lost childhood that felt suffocated by the oppression of the enemy. Whatever got buried in the rubble, God lifts the heaviness to bring joy where our heart was once burdened. Our help, joy, and peace are on the way; it will not tarry. Wait for it...wait for it...then, BAM. Suddenly, it appears like *Emeril* Lagasse as God "kicks it up a notch" on our behalf. According to the prophet Isaiah, those who trust God will be restored.

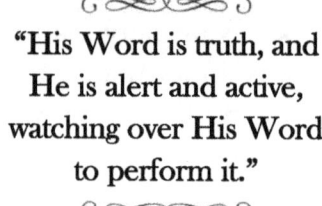

"His Word is truth, and He is alert and active, watching over His Word to perform it."

His comfort rings loud and clear. "Do not earnestly remember the former things; neither consider the things of old. Behold, I am doing a new thing! Now it springs forth; do you not perceive and know it and will you not give heed to it? I will even make a way in the wilderness and rivers in the desert" (Isaiah 43:18, AMPC).

Bonus Number 15

The number 15 in my dream had another added bonus, and though I dealt with my struggle with fear more in-depth in Chapter 5, since this one relates to my dream, I wanted to touch on it again here.

Whenever we stayed in a hotel room, I preferred it no higher than the second floor. While at our stay, 99.9 % of the time, I would take the stairs, jokingly saying I need my exercise as I ascend the steps, knowing the underlying issue is really fear-based, not the cherry dipped cone from Dairy Queen I had consumed earlier. Truth is, I was really afraid of getting stuck in elevators. It's funny coming from a girl who did cartwheels in the Montgomery Ward elevator repeatedly when I was supposed to be selling

Camp Fire Girl thin mints at Mall 205 with my friend.

When my cardio up the flights of stairs was completed and I entered our room, fear number two came upon me like a BFF who won't do a cartwheel. The first thing I did was drop my bags down and head to the window. Not to see the beautiful view but to look for an escape plan in case of a fire. I know, right? Lord have mercy...

My mind began to calculate how many bedsheets one needs to shimmy down to freedom. At that point, neither high thread count nor softness matters. When it comes to survival, my goal is for them to just hold up so I can get down.

So, in all the excitement with getting our room for the Lavish Conference, when the room key came with the 15th floor, I looked at my friend and said, "That is a lot of bed sheets if we have a fire." She looked at me and said, "I never thought of that." I wanted to say, "Well, you better; we have lots of sheets to tie together, girlfriend." Maybe even add a 'chop chop' with a hand clap to emphasize my sense of urgency.

And don't even get me started on the 15 flights of stairs; I realized my friend would not want to walk with her sore knee. I was not sure I even wanted to do that myself. I was in a predicament, to say the least. At this time, I had nowhere to go but up, and luckily for me, I packed a pair of big-girl pants for the weekend. I had a feeling I would be stretched during my stay.

However, it was not my fancy big-girl pants that got me through; it was my big God. Where would we be without Him? I, for one, would be stuck on the second floor, tying sheets after my winding climb up the stairs. Thankfully, we serve an incredibly loving God who cheers us on to overcome our fears for the win.

"Everything we could ever need for life and complete devotion to God has already been deposited in us by his divine power. For all this was lavished upon us through the rich experience of knowing him who has called us by name and invited us to come to him through a glorious manifestation of his goodness" (2 Peter 1:3, TPT).

That day, as I looked out the window of the 15th floor, I leaned into God, learning to trust my Father for safety, because my plan A of knotting sheets was not an option at this height! Instead, the right plan was B, and that was to be still and know He is God, which is always the best plan ever. As I gazed out that window of letting go and letting God, I soaked in a breathtaking view of the stunning Mt. Hood and downtown Portland, Oregon, in a whole new way. I was right in the heart of the city where I was born and raised, living only a stone's throw away from ever since. It was a view I would have totally missed by looking down and trying to survive rather than to thrive.

"This resurrection life you received from God is not a timid, grave tending life. It's adventurously expectant, greeting God with a childlike 'What's next, Papa?' God's Spirit touches our spirits and confirms who we really are. We know who he is, and we know who we are: Father and children. And we know we are going to get what's coming to us—an unbelievable inheritance! We go through exactly what Christ goes through. If we go through the hard times with him, then we're certainly going to go through the good times with him! (Romans 8 15-17, MSG).

Throughout my life, I have let sorrow, loss, regret, and fear take the reins instead of fully allowing Jesus to rule and reign supremely over my life. I'm so thankful I do not have to live like that any longer, and neither do you.

"I hear the Lord saying, 'I will stay close to you,
instructing and guiding you along the pathway for your life.
I will advise you along the way
and lead you forth with my eyes as your guide.
So don't make it difficult; don't be stubborn
when I take you where you've not been before.
Don't make me tug you and pull you along.
Just come with me!'" —Psalm 32:8-9, TPT

Closed Doors, Opened Windows

For all the years I have heard the phrase *when God closes a door, He opens a window.* Though I quoted it, I never really liked it. To me, a window was smaller than a door. Right there, it's clear my thinking toward God's goodness was off base, until recently when the thought of this saying came to mind. I heard the Lord say, "Why do you think windows are smaller than doors?" It actually jolted my thinking, as He then brought to mind the glorious windows I had seen the day before at a transitional youth home called Harmony House. The window views were open wide and expansive, and the story of love and provision for that miracle home was even more impressive.

It was there where I more fully realized that God was not limiting me; rather, I was limiting God. Looking back, I'm still baffled at the lie I was blinded by, but today I thank God. The truth is, I once was blind and now I see the wide-open window view that is, indeed, spectacular.

From Our *Whys* To God's Wonder

What Is Your View?

Take some time to ask the Lord to help you with your views on the topics below. Allow time to listen to the Lord and write down your feelings. There is no wrong answer; it is you getting to know yourself and your loving Heavenly Father.

You may find you want more space to write your thoughts using an accompanying journal or sketchbook, which are so rewarding.

View of God

_____
_____
_____

View of Yourself

_____
_____
_____

View on Life

_____
_____
_____

The Lord wants to give you a room with a beautiful view – an upgrade, remodel, addition to your existing joy. He'll take you places your feet have never touched, with such divine healing and transformation; comforting areas to suit your grieving heart, bringing the seemingly untouchable with a divine touch of wholeness. Jesus brings to you His good tiding of great joy. That is a view we never want to miss.

*"Then he broke through and transformed all my wailing
into a whirling dance of ecstatic praise!
He has torn the veil and lifted from me
the sad heaviness of mourning.
He wrapped me in the glory garments of gladness.
How could I be silent when it's time to praise you?
Now my heart sings out loud, bursting with joy—
a bliss inside that keeps me singing,
I can never thank you enough!"* —Psalm 30:11 TPT

"...you ripped off my black mourning band and decked me with wildflowers. I'm about to burst with song..." —Psalm 30:11, MSG

"Just when the caterpillar thought the world was over, it became a butterfly." —Chuang Tzu

"I have learned more from pain than I could've ever learned from pleasure." —Unknown Author

"My mission in life is not merely to survive, but to thrive; and to do so with some passion, some compassion, some humor, and some style."
—Maya Angelou

"Collect wages from your grief work. God's Decree..."
—Jeremiah 31:17, MSG

Reclaiming Prayer

Abba Father, we thank You for changing us and our view from glory to glory. At times in the process, it does not feel glorious at all but quite painful. You are fully invested in our healing and freedom that sets the captives free, and those You set free are free indeed. Your Word tells us to look up for that hope.

"So if the Son sets you free, you will be absolutely free" (John 8:36 GW).

"And at last, when you see how the Son of Man comes—surrounded with a cloud, with great power and miracles, in the radiance of his splendor, and with great glory and praise—it will make you jump for joy! For the day of your full transformation has arrived" (Luke 21:27-28, TPT).

We stand in agreement for our healing. On earth as it is in Heaven. Thank You, Jesus.

Final Thoughts

Healing's Patchwork Quilt

*"Your inheritance in the land will be doubled
and your joy go on forever."*
—Isaiah 61:7 (MSG)

Once an excavation site has been decided, they clear the debris to make a rectangular grid, marking off the area, resembling patches on a quilt if we use our imagination. Each section is now able to gently begin the uncovering of buried artifacts while documenting their finds. When I look back on my journey of healing, I had precious people in my life who set the groundwork for my freedom. These were ever so patient, ready to roll their sleeves up to fight for me.

One grid was my committed and faithful husband loving me enough to uncover the deeply embedded lies of feeling unlovable. Another grid was our precious sons who loved me unconditionally out of the rubble with love and forgiveness in difficult and trying circumstances. My precious mentors and friends, far too many to count, saw hope and redemption under all the wreckage and held my hand along the way. The grid of my mother taught me to love God with all my heart since childhood; it also taught me the value and sheer necessity of prayer, which is a vital lifeline to my broken spirit.

My quilt is still being made with up-to-date, colorful squares of healing to explore new relationships; relationships like my beautiful daughter-in-love Erin and our precious grandchildren who add brand new thrilling adventures and different ways to see things. Today, I'm even thankful for the rubble I was once buried under, because I saw God like I would never have otherwise.

May the Lord expand our thankfulness as we walk away from this time holy and humbled by His goodness and love toward us. Let us pursue wholeness like water and the very air we breathe, inhaling the breath of God as our spirit revives. His living water quenches our parched soul like none other. As we cling to our Heavenly Father, we welcome all the resources He lays before us. In due time, we will find buried treasure and untapped potential of restored joy under the rubble of life's circumstances. He is calling us not to despair and lean into His glorious promise.

Let us pursue wholeness like water and the very air we breathe.

"The mighty Spirit of Lord Yahweh is wrapped around me Because Yahweh has anointed me, as a messenger to preach good news to the poor He sent me to heal the wounds of the brokenhearted, to tell captives, 'You are free,' and to tell prisoners, 'Be free from your darkness.' I am sent to announce a new season of Yahweh's grace and a time of God's recompense on his enemies, to comfort all who are in sorrow, to strengthen those crushed by despair who mourn in Zion—to give them a beautiful bouquet in the place of ashes, the oil of bliss instead of tears, and the mantle of joyous praise instead of the spirit of heaviness. Because of this, they will be known as Mighty Oaks of Righteousness, planted by Yahweh as a living display of his glory. They will restore ruins from long ago and rebuild what was long devastated. They will renew ruined cities and desolation of past generations.

Foreigners will be appointed to shepherd your many flocks; strangers will cultivate your fields and tend your vines, Messiah's Ministers But you will be known as Priests of Yahweh, and called Servants of our God. You will feast on the wealth of nations and revel in their riches! Because you received a double dose of shame and dishonor, **you will inherit a double portion of endless joy and everlasting bliss!** For I, Yahweh, love fairness and justice, and I hate stealing and sin. I will rightly repay them because of my faithfulness and enter into an everlasting covenant with them. Their seed will be famous among the nations, and their descendants the center of attention of the people. All who see them will recognize that they are the seed that Yahweh has blessed with favor!" (Isaiah 61:1-9, TPT).

And last but not least, don't forget your precious acorn promise...

The Forgotten Acorn

Many years ago, while strolling down the sidewalk of the mall with my mama and two little ones, we found ourselves inside a craft store. Even to this day, my heart skips a beat with excitement. Immersing myself in the creativity that flows from talented employees and stunning decorative products is always delightful. Though I rarely purchase much, my eyes feast to their fill in endless imaginative possibilities.

That particular day was no exception. Winding around the aisles with wonder, we stopped at the unfinished wood section. Derek, our excited three-year-old, knelt down to get a closer look at the bountiful supply of wooden objects. Quickly, his hands and mind burgeoned with inventiveness, gazing at the wooden wheels, round orbs, and dowels, to name a few of the vast assortment. As our visit came to a close, he lifted his knees from the dusty floor and bid adieu to the wooden kingdom he ruled over momentarily. The little king left his temporary abode, and unbeknownst to me, he left behind the little wooden acorn he brought with him to the store. Overcome with endless options, he laid down his tiny acorn treasure to grab ahold of something new and more intriguing.

This small, carved wooden acorn was a gift I bought my husband before we were married. It was a beautiful reminder that a small, seemingly insignificant acorn is really a cleverly disguised full-grown oak tree. It heralds the importance of not despising small beginnings, for God always sees the bigger picture. So much so that all the potentials of a mighty oak is in a nut that cradles a seed of stately greatness. This tiny acorn captivated our son's attention, and though at the time he did not understand its deeper significance, it still became a beloved trinket he faithfully carried around as a child.

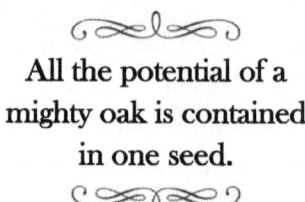

All the potential of a mighty oak is contained in one seed.

Months came and went without notice of the little nut that went AWOL. In all our busyness of life, the acorn dropped off everyone's radars. Winter had passed, and the promise of spring was now replacing barren branches; new life burst through bleak soil and dreary skies. Spring now welcoming us out of winters' hibernation, wooing us to celebrate its arrival, it was a perfect time to get out of the house. So, we wasted no time loading up the kids in Mom's car to run an errand to the Oregon City Mall.

Upon arrival, we happily greeted the outdoor sidewalks that were now doable without the winter chill. We were taking in all the sights and sounds as we moseyed down the path of the mall toward the craft store. Out of the blue, Derek blurted out, "My acorn, my acorn!" Mom and I looked at each other, realizing in unison he had left his little acorn in an ocean of unfinished wood pieces months before. Though apprehensive, we prayed that what was lost would be found. As you now know, my mom was good at that.

Mom and I picked up the pace with Trent, our youngest, in the stroller, positioning ourselves to be his wingman while he ran with a mission to get there ASAP. Racing to the wooden wonderland he once ruled over, he quickly bent down, this time, in hopes to find what he had left behind. Lo and behold, to all of our astonishment, his little acorn lay right where he had left it months earlier. Squealing with delight, he reclaimed his lost treasure, grasping it tightly with an unwavering resolve of ownership and relief. Mom and I, too, were relieved, rejoicing because what was lost had eventually been found.

That little wooden acorn survived both customers' and employees' restocking, remaining an undisturbed, holy treasure hidden in plain view, its meaning, purpose, and truth laid down but not lost forever. Dormant, yet brimming with life's fullness, it waited to be unleashed and reclaimed.

I don't know about you, but in times past, I, too, have laid down things in order to grab what caught my attention or piqued my curiosity. In doing so, letting go of an important treasure allured by a possible worthy contender. There were times in my life when my faith in God was laid on a shelf while I chose to walk away. Deep wounds were seemingly too painful to endure without the help of worldly distractions to fill the unholy chasm. At times, I turned my back on God, perhaps believing He had turned His back on me. My purpose, self-worth, and destiny remained fallow as I grappled with a pain that no worldly possession was able to soothe. That is until a day came when, in all my restlessness and emptiness, a realization finally dawned on me.

God not only loves us unconditionally, but He also patiently waits for the seed of greatness He planted in all of us to take root. Though I had temporarily left that truth on a shelf like my son's acorn, He remains steadfast, offering a future and a hope that does not disappoint. His seed of promise bursts with breathtaking grandeur, unlimited potential, and more brouhaha than anything the world has to offer. The funny thing is, the Hebrew meaning of brouhaha is *blessed be he who enters*. And to think I just found it fun to say!

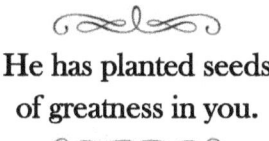

He has planted seeds of greatness in you.

So, no matter how far you strayed away, or how unworthy you feel for the choices you made along the way, God bids you enter and be blessed. His Word paints for us a soul-comforting picture of unyielding commitment. My prayer is that you and I run back to God with all the zeal our son had when he finally realized what he forgot and embrace the joy in the glorious rediscovery. God is in the business of finding and being found, and you are no exception. His deepest longing is to reclaim the irreplaceable treasure called YOU. That, my friend, is a big deal, or as I like to say, a whole lotta brouhaha!

"The creation of a thousand forests is in one acorn."
—Ralph Waldo Emerson

Perhaps you are yet to accept Jesus as your personal Savior. You can do this right now by asking Jesus to come into your heart as your Lord and Savior, asking Him to forgive you.

If you prayed, I'm so proud of your decision to accept Jesus as your Lord and Savior. You are deeply and profoundly loved.

Reclaimed Joy has a companion journal available with all the verses used in the book for easy access. Visit www.LisasJourney.net for more information and ordering links.

Lisa's blog: visit **www.LisasJourney.net**

Follow Lisa on Instagram: **@heartfulministries**

Connect with Lisa on Facebook: **Lisa Thompson Jennings**

To contact Lisa with reader testimonials, interview requests or to book her for a speaking opportunity, contact her now at **lisathompsonjennings@gmail.com**

If you've enjoyed this book, please consider leaving *Reclaimed Joy* a positive review on Amazon and Goodreads!

Published with help from 100X Publishing:

www.ingramcontent.com/pod-product-compliance
Lightning Source LLC
Chambersburg PA
CBHW051759040426
42446CB00007B/436